Harvesting Hope

with

Anthony de Mello

JOHN CALLANAN SJ

First published in 2017 by
coluмвα press

23 Merrion Square
Dublin 2, Ireland
www.Columba.ie

Copyright © 2017 John Callanan SJ

ISBN: 978-1-78218-321-1

Set in Freight Text Pro 10/13
Cover and book design by Alba Esteban | Columba Press
Front cover photograph by Aleksandar Grozdanovski from Shutterstock
Printed by Jellyfish Solutions

Harvesting Hope

with

Anthony de Mello

JOHN CALLANAN SJ

columba press

I dedicate this book to the memory of my parents,
John R. Callanan and Una Kelly
And to the members of my family
And my fellow Jesuits

CONTENTS

LIST OF PRAYER EXERCISES AND MEDITATIONS

ACKNOWLEDGEMENTS

I am greatly indebted to David Gaffney SJ and Eddie O'Donnell SJ for their kindness and skill in checking over the text and correcting grammar and any other errors that made their way into the material. It's a painstaking task. The errors that remain are my own.

Dublin 2017

FOREWORD

This is the fifth book I've written about Anthony de Mello. You may well ask, 'Why write another?' My answer is short and simple. I loved listening to the man myself and found most of what he had to say about prayer really helpful. I do not know anyone in the last thirty years who has had a bigger influence on the way I try to pray. That statement is true also for many I come into contact with who are attempting to improve their own prayer lives. De Mello's enthusiasm and energy infused many and encouraged them to reintroduce prayer into their lives. This book hopes to do the same.

Fr de Mello was an Indian priest, retreat-giver and prayer guru. He was also a member of a Catholic religious order – the Society of Jesus – and he achieved international fame for his writings and spiritual retreats. During his life, he often mentioned that God speaks to us. That may not be a particularly unusual concept in itself, but in Fr de Mello's hands it took on new meaning. It became alive and concrete. 'Wake up' was his message, for he claimed that most of us make our way through life in a 'sleep-like' state. He was a master storyteller and mixed his tales with illustrations from everyday life to make his lessons vibrant and fascinating. His words highlighted the fact that you or I may become aware of God's presence if we take the time to tune in to what is going on within and around us.

As the years go by, I seem to meet more and more people who find it difficult to pray. In their lives, God seems to be missing – but not missed. They have problems about how they should face life and the trials and tribulations that it invariably throws up. Their difficulties come in all sorts of areas. Either their lives are too long or too short. Their pace of life is too frenetic or not frenzied enough. They feel burdened with trying to survive on too little money – or too much. They puzzle over why they are on earth at all and ask themselves what the purpose of their existence is. Trying to attain balance and happiness in their lives seems to be beyond them. The questions are neither original nor unusual and Anthony de Mello was asked them often enough in his own time. How he answered seemed to inspire those who came into contact with him, for his thoughts and talks on prayer helped millions.

His ideas created waves – not least within Church circles – but his books and videos have provided hope and inspiration to many. His ministry was short-lived. While preparing to deliver a workshop on prayer in New York in 1987, he died suddenly of a heart attack. That's thirty years ago, so you may wonder why he continues to inspire Christians today or why material about him still proliferates. I find that his story and his ideas – about prayer and life – still strike a chord with many. I hope this book will do the same for you.

INTRODUCTION

Fr Anthony de Mello first came to Ireland in 1977. Not much was known about him then – at least not in any of the circles I moved in. However, shortly after his arrival, he conducted his first retreat in our country and a number of Irish Jesuits – of whom I was lucky to be one – attended. The goings-on left a deep impression on me then – and the memory of it still warms the cockles of my heart. De Mello began his input with a personal story that obviously meant a lot to him. He mentioned one red-letter day in his life when an event had taken place that would always stand out for him and leave an indelible mark. The episode, he told us, took place in India just after he was ordained. An elderly priest who looked like he was at the end of his tether asked him to take over his confessional for a short period because the old man was exhausted and needed someone to stand in for him. As de Mello sat down he admitted that he felt really holy. For three hours he laboured in the darkness and when he finally came out of the confessional he was downright depressed. That bothered him, so he tried to discover what the cause of his gloom might be. As he related the story to us, he admitted that it took him some little time to find out why he felt depressed.

'Basically,' he said, 'I wasn't being true to myself in that box and I knew that's never good. I was giving those who came along to the confessional a lot of pious platitudes. Nothing desperately wrong with that, I suppose, but as I thought about it I knew I was robbing them of something much more valuable. I gave them what I had been taught throughout the years of my studies, but not what I myself practised and found useful in my own prayer life.' De Mello then went on to reveal slowly but surely the things that he did find really rich and profitable during his own prayer periods. It's those insights that hit home so forcibly when I first heard him speak and it is those same pearls of wisdom that we shall try to get to the heart of as we journey through this book.

But who was this Anthony de Mello? He was born on 4 September 1931, in a village near the city of Mumbai, to pious Catholic parents. In Ireland, we usually referred to him as 'Tony' instead of Anthony, so if I refer to him as Tony throughout the book I hope you will forgive me. He himself said that some of his faith enthusiasm and insights were most probably given to him during his earliest childhood experiences and he had many spiritual reasons to be grateful to his family. His early faith memories were positive and his household gave him a firm and confident religious base. From this position he was able, in faith terms, to explore and search. It allowed him, in later life, to look with confidence into his cultural background and it left him unafraid to mine the riches of the Hindu and Buddhist traditions of his native India. His writings suggest that these factors had an important influence on much of his later thinking.

Finishing school at the early age of sixteen, he joined the Society of Jesus and began his Jesuit training. As is the way with religious formation in the Society, he followed a set regime. I suspect that this regime did not vary much whether you were in India or Ireland. To begin with, one completes a two-year noviceship. Much of this is spent in prayer and silence. It has at least two purposes. It is designed to allow aspirants decide whether the Jesuit way of life is right for them and it also allows the Society of Jesus to form an opinion as to the suitability of the candidate for the order.

The Years of Study

Those first two years of tranquillity and decision-making are followed by something completely different – formal study – and lots of it. De Mello was sent to read philosophy in Barcelona, psychology at Loyola University in Chicago and theology at the Gregorian University in Rome. During this time, he acquired a taste for Christian mystical spirituality – most notably the insights of St Ignatius of Loyola, St Teresa of Avila and St John of the Cross. When he later added a psychological dimension to his thinking during time spent in Loyola University, Chicago, the basis of his prayer style was set in place. Shrewd observers noted that his fusion of psychological insights, concentrating as they do on the strengths and weaknesses of human nature, was counter-balanced by the concept of human good and evil contained in eastern and western spirituality. Such a mixture was always capable of producing a heady cocktail, and in de Mello's case, it certainly did.

As a Teacher

De Mello set the cat among the pigeons when it came to looking at the whole area of spiritual development and growth. He had the rare gift of bringing vitality and spiritual energy wherever he went. It coursed through his veins and sparkled out of him as soon as he opened his mouth. He began by encouraging silence, because he believed that inner stillness brought clarity. As he often mentioned, 'muddy waters, if they're let become still, begin to clear'. Along with the silence, he encouraged 'awareness'. Stay in the here and now and try and notice what is 'going on', both in yourself and in how you are relating to your environment. He didn't say this was easy. As a starter, he would advise participants at his workshops to undertake an experiment and suggested that they take up a bodily prayer posture they were comfortable with. They should then lightly close their eyes and maintain silence for a period of ten minutes or thereabouts. They might begin by soaking themselves in the silence and see what revelation it might bring. At the end of the ten minutes he often invited the participants to share with the others present what each had experienced during their quiet time. Sometimes group members found it helpful to jot down their insights on paper before they began to relate them verbally. This exercise didn't take long, and most found it fun. That was part of de Mello's talent.

At Workshops

Participants in the workshops found de Mello explaining that his goal as an educator was to change people, not just their ideas. In fact he hoped that those who took part in his seminars might decide to change themselves. First they had some exploring to do. As many great masters tell us, some of life's most important questions centre upon the general areas of 'Who am I? What principles do I live my life by? Where have I picked up those principles and are they solid? If not, would the pain involved in effecting a change be possible for me to bear – and would it be worth the effort?'

First Visit to Ireland

Irish Jesuits first got a taste of these insights in 1977. The provincial of the order in Ireland had participated in the General Congregation of the Society of Jesus in Rome and had attended prayer sessions that de Mello had been asked to conduct there. Greatly enthused, the Irish provincial asked his Indian confrère to come to Ireland to present a prayer workshop to Jesuits the following summer. The event duly took place and about sixty Irish Jesuits attended. They didn't know what they had let themselves in for. Almost as soon as de Mello arrived, those present could feel electricity in the air. I myself, just finished my Jesuit noviceship, was lucky enough to get one of the last remaining vacant places and was bowled over by the experience. It quickly became obvious that what de Mello was about to say would be both challenging and life-changing. He explained that the sessions he was about to present would be grounded in his own experience. To illustrate this he recounted how, shortly after he was ordained, he had been sent to a house of formation for Indian novices and asked to give them lectures on prayer. To his mind, this would be a more-or-less straightforward task – but it turned out to be anything but. Some of the self-revelation that occurred meant that Tony himself had to change his fundamental beliefs about what the practice of prayer could or should be like in his own life.

Teaching the Novices

As de Mello explained to us, he started his spiritual inputs with the novices as any conscientious and reasonable individual might do. He stuck to the script and presented ideas about prayer as he himself had been taught them. When questions began to come from his audience, he realised that his teaching was seriously deficient. He found he was presenting his lessons in textbook fashion and he somehow sensed that his students were less than impressed. The theory he was giving out was solid enough – but therein lay a problem. It was just theory. He was regurgitating what he himself had been taught but was neither presenting nor following what he knew to be true from his own prayer practice. He thus began to formulate a very important principle for himself. Henceforth, he would test each prayer practice or principle before he presented it to his students. He would, in a sense, be like a goldsmith, testing his theories in the light and fire of his own prayer experience. In this way he would see if the prayer practices he recommended really stood up to the rigours of daily life. He would scrape, polish and analyse each scrap of material that arose during his own prayer time and see what the events were saying to him. Only then – after he had seen if the practices proved to be personally profitable – would he present them to his students. He found that some of the prayer methods he had previously practised and spoken about were less effective and truthful than they might have been. As a goldsmith might have put it, some of those practices were base metal. He resolved that from that point onwards he would speak only from his own personal prayer experience.

De Mello's Work in Sadhana

That ability and willingness to examine what worked in his own prayer life deeply influenced and benefited de Mello. His ability as a speaker and teacher developed rapidly. Before long, he was sent to head up a retreat centre, Sadhana, near Bombay. Here, the basic honesty of his approach in matters of prayer proved immensely popular and his seminars and retreats were much sought after. In part because of a need to finance the retreats themselves, but also to keep Sadhana afloat, de Mello spent a good part of every summer conducting seminars and workshops in Europe, North America, the Philippines, Australia and Japan. He also visited Ireland. Large crowds were the order of the day. Those who attended were dazzled by his wit and wisdom. He was a magical storyteller, but each story – a little like Christ's stories in the gospels – had a clear and profound message. Participants at the seminars were invited, in the usual de Mello style, to examine the principles they lived by. What were their core values? Were those values really true? How strongly would they hold up in the heat of the goldsmith's fire?

Controversy

All this, of course, was controversial. De Mello himself told us during his Irish visits that Sadhana had been visited twice to see if it was holding to a strictly orthodox line. He knew that in life he created something of a storm. In death he has done the same. On the one hand, his vigour and freshness in faith matters instantly stimulate those who read his books, listen to his audio presentations or watch his videos. On the other hand, because his presentations were so fresh, new and challenging, some people were bound to be outraged. Most realised that he had a special gift: not only for presenting spiritual ideas that might sustain them – but for doing so in an invigorating and enlightened manner.

There is a second side to this story that should, in honesty, be spoken about. Some segments of the Church hierarchy have, from time to time, been less than enthusiastic about de Mello's teaching. In June 1998, the Vatican Congregation for the Doctrine of the Faith put these misgivings into print. They went so far as to issue a sort of 'Government Health Warning' about de Mello's work. A notification was sent to all bishops warning that de Mello and his teachings might be injurious to those that read them. Numerous reviews and articles reported this notification. Interestingly, few seemed to agree with it, and fewer still considered that the arguments carried serious weight. The majority of commentators, both then and subsequently, suggested that those who were having trouble with de Mello and his wisdom did not fully understand the eastern mindset.

The Objections

It's hard to pinpoint exactly which elements of de Mello's work disturbed those who objected, but three issues seemed to be uppermost in their minds. As I understand it, they wondered, firstly, if de Mello mistakenly equated God with nature. I have some difficulty understanding where they got this idea from. In his videos, de Mello does speak of God and nature being like the dancer and the dance. They are not the same, but they are closely intertwined. Many people, it seemed to de Mello, discovered glimpses of God in the beauty that surrounds them. You might say that the splendour of nature gives us a hint and possibly some vague idea of the beauty of God.

Secondly, the Congregation for the Doctrine of the Faith wondered whether de Mello gave due deference to belief in the divinity of Jesus. They pondered whether he really highlighted the fact that Jesus was the Son of God, or just put Jesus on a par with other great prophets. Where they got this idea from I have no idea. Certainly if one looks at his videos it is hard to see how this impression could arise, for those who watch are normally struck by the great reverence that de Mello attaches to the second person of the Trinity.

Finally, the Congregation seemed to think that de Mello did not show sufficient deference to the institution of the Church itself. Here I think Anthony de Mello himself might plead partially guilty. A warm and generous feeling towards one's own Church is both admirable and wise, but slavishly following any church or organisation uncritically does it no favours. As the Irish Church has discovered to its cost, if an institution is unable or unwilling to examine itself constructively from within, then its enemies – and even neutral observers - will do so from without. Uncritical silence in such situations, I suspect, is not faithfulness, but unhelpful cowardice. Great love demands great honesty.

His Final Days

The punishing schedule of year-long work in the Sadhana prayer centre, coupled with a summer menu of retreats and workshops abroad, took its toll. His last retreat, and the one that finally stilled his incessant enthusiasm for life, was held at Fordham University in New York in June 1987. His heart finally gave out during that retreat. His work and spirit, however, did not die with him.

In retrospect we can see that Anthony de Mello touched and radically altered the lives of many. They found in his writings and his thought a heady cocktail of sense and inspiration in matters of prayer and they thus refuse to let his name be forgotten. At a Zen centre in California some little time ago, the lecturer, Suen Sa Nim, was asked a long, rambling and almost incomprehensible question by one of his audience. After quite a long silence, Suen gave his reply. All he said to his questioner was, 'You're crazy'. As you can imagine, there was a moment of stunned silence. The audience held its breath as tension rose. Then Suen Sa Nim smiled and finished his sentence. 'But you're not crazy enough.' I think Anthony de Mello might have felt the same way about the attitude we should take.

A Note on The Prayer Exercises

At the end of each chapter I will provide at least three prayer exercises which you might like to try. Generally, the first will be a breathing exercise, which will prepare you for entering into a prayerful space (this breathing exercise is repeated several times throughout the book). The second offering will usually be a gospel meditation, some viewed from different perspectives. Many of the gospel scenes are suitable for prayer, and in our formative years as Jesuits this was the way we were normally advised to pray. Finally, Anthony de Mello himself often used a style of prayer that many describe as 'fantasy'. The third offering will usually be presented in that format.

1

WHAT IS PRAYER?

Prayer is an expression of who we are.
Thomas Merton

A student intending to take on doctoral studies at Princeton once asked, 'What is there left in the world for original dissertation research?' Albert Einstein replied, 'Find out about prayer. Somebody must find out about prayer.'

The late Fr Anthony de Mello, an Indian Jesuit priest and prayer guru, is a writer and speaker I'm very fond of. As you listen to his audio material or watch his videos, a number of subject areas are touched on. One is the suggestion that we should try to discover God in all things and in all human experiences in which we are engaged, so let's begin our exploration of prayer there.

Recently I met up with a religious sister, a friend of mine. She had just come back to Ireland from Africa and she may have thought that she had left that continent, but it certainly hadn't left her. Her conversation was littered with anecdotes about the people she lived with and the way they touched her life. She is a primary school teacher, and many of her memories are about the children she taught and the escapades they got up to. One of her teaching memories really touched a chord in me and throws a light on what prayer may be about.

Last Christmas, she was teaching an infants class in her African school. As the school was putting on a Nativity play, she and her group were asked to begin the evening's festivities with some music to entertain the parents. Even though they were only four or five years of age, the children were asked to bring the evening's proceedings to a close with some suitable musical choice of their own. After some discussion, the class decided they should finish with the *'The Little Drummer Boy'*. You'll remember the piece. It has a good steady rhythm and simple words – perfect for the age group my friend worked with. The class would easily remember the words. As an added attraction it was decided that the smallest lad in the class – a four-year-old who couldn't sing, but who looked like an angel – would be the star of the piece. He would be placed in front and beat out the song's tempo on a drum.

The plan looked easy enough. As rehearsals got under way, my friend stayed out of the limelight but honed the performance to perfection. She explained to one and all what she was looking for and told them that only their very best endeavours would be good enough. Each child was reminded that they were showcasing the school's talents and reputation. They were also reminded that, as junior 'professionals', they should keep their minds on the job and not become distracted. Despite the fact that relatives would be present, these were not to be waved at – or even noticed – while the performance was going on. At last, the night of the great event arrived.

Excitement was intense. From early evening, relatives came by car, bicycle, and even on foot. No one wanted to miss the presentation. Extra seating had to be called for. Various dignitaries sat in the front row; the reverend mother, local political figures, even the bishop. Everything went exactly as planned and the Nativity play was a roaring success. The finale of the evening was at hand. My friend's young choir waited in the wings, hopping from foot to foot with anticipation. The announcer informed the audience that they had one final treat. The infant group's big moment had arrived. With grace and pride my friend ushered her young charges out onto the stage and held her breath.

The group – and their song – began. At first quietly, but then with greater insistence, the small boy and his drum began to pound out a beat. All was going perfectly but, as they say in the trade, 'it's wise never to work on stage with children or animals'. Without warning or explanation, her leading light – the little drummer boy – lost his concentration. His drumming began to fade. As she looked on from the wings, she noticed his demeanour had changed. The lad had clearly forgotten where he was and was beginning to peer out from the brightly lit stage into the darkened hall. He shielded his eyes from the lights as his gaze swept from left to right. With increasing desperation, he tried to pick out his mother from the many dimly lit figures seated in front of him. He could make out very little in the semi-darkness. He certainly couldn't see any sign of his mother and his eyes and whole body expressed his desperation. He took a step forward and made one last effort to spot his mother amid the gloom – without success. Great big tears ran down his face. At that exact moment, the singing behind him stopped. The choir had done its duty, but our four-year-old drummer boy was completely oblivious. From above, the stage curtain began to descend. As the wave of applause began, the curtain came down neatly in front of the rest of the choir as they made their bow. Isolated before the drapes, our hero was left there in front on his own, tears running down his face, completely abandoned. In his eyes, his mother had failed to turn up.

As my friend, the religious sister, tells it, there was a completely different vantage point from where she stood. Looking on from the wings during that last act, the stage lights had not dazzled her. From where she stood, she could make out figures in the hall pretty clearly. Right at the back, a woman was going frantic. She was the young drummer's mother and she was waving with all her might. It was as if she was crying out, 'I'm here, I'm here', and trying to let her young son know she was present. With everything she had she was demonstrating that she was there for him – she would always be there for him. He need have no worries. As a postscript, the sister said to me that, for her, it was a bit like God and a representation of how God works in the world. He's there, in relationship, behind or around us, supporting, loving and ever-present – even if we fail to notice.

Maybe that story can explain a little about prayer in our lives. Many of us wonder what prayer is and how we might go about establishing contact with God. Is it about God speaking to us? Perhaps it's about our ability – or inability – to listen. Does God really speak to us? If so, when does he speak, where does he speak, how and through whom, and how should we respond to his promptings?

To find answers these questions, it might be worth looking initially at what I suspect are a number of false notions about prayer. To illustrate, I should first mention that I work in a university and the first type of 'bogus prayer' one is often asked to engage in is what I might term the 'Lester Piggott' school of petition. Now Lester Piggott is a very famous British jockey, now retired. He won everything, and many people used to say, 'Hail Mary, full of grace, Lester Piggott win the race'. Students on the eve of exams often come along to their college chaplain and mention that they are terrified when they think about the events they will shortly have to face. Could the chaplain pray for the success of their forthcoming exams? As you might expect, I'm happy to do what I can in this regard and usually ask what subject they are sitting and how things have gone during the year. 'I hate the subject and could never bear to go to the lectures,' they say. That's the exam they are asking prayers for. Now that's a sort of 'Lester Piggott' petition in my book. They are doing nothing to aid they own case but hope God will do all the work and somehow produce a miracle. That does not seem like a fair deal. It absolves the person involved of responsibility and puts much of the onus on God. The opposite extreme – keeping God out of the equation – seems equally unsatisfactory. I heard recently about a man who came to the university because he had arranged an important interview there. The meeting was set for ten o'clock but the poor guy found all the car parks full when he arrived. He drove around in desperation as the ten o'clock deadline came closer. Finally, in utter desperation, he shouted up to the heavens, 'Lord, if you find me a place to park I'll go to Mass every morning for the rest of the month.' Almost on cue, as he rounded the corner, he found a gent pulling his car out of a spot. Nipping into the space, our driver shouts into the sky again, 'Never mind, never mind, the deal is off. I've found a space myself.' Not giving thanks for the favours we receive is not at all uncommon. Failing to put in the effort is one of the things that prayer is not.

To say what it is – well that's another matter altogether. Some spiritual writers say it is a raising up of the mind and heart to God. Certainly, some form of communication between God and ourselves seems to be involved. For such communication to happen, silence may be a prerequisite, for it builds up a necessary quiet space within us, and the tranquillity thus gained helps us think about who, where and how we are. This leads to a greater awareness about what has been going on in our lives and encourages us to return to places and experiences that have proved helpful in the past. It also helps us to notice where God may have been revealing himself to us.

Anthony de Mello regularly asked us to create such space within ourselves for reflection. In doing this he was only following the dictum of St Ignatius of Loyola, the founder of the Jesuits, who suggested that we go back to such places in our imagination in order to gain enlightenment. Ignatius recommended that, at regular intervals, we might look back at experiences given to us in life and chew over lessons learnt, before looking at how we might most wisely move forward. While looking backwards, we should try to notice where the Lord may have been close in times past and ask ourselves where we have found Christ in times of pain or joy. Strangely enough, looking back at our past failures can be even more fruitful than glorying in any successes. The frustrations, anger, sadness, confusion and discouragement of past failures may have lessons for me and create a climate that reveals where the Lord is trying to lead me. To pinpoint these lessons, however, requires taking time out to ponder – as both St Ignatius and de Mello were continually pointing out. Both spoke repeatedly about the advisability of stepping back from our busy schedules at regular intervals in order to review and work out what's going on within us, to pause and see if an insight or a particular grace is being offered. If God is speaking, our chances of noticing are greatly enhanced if we remain vigilant and silent.

To underscore this, I find a story from the life of Cecil Rhodes very illuminating. Rhodes, as you may remember, was an explorer of great courage and energy who gave his name to the African country, Rhodesia, now known as Zimbabwe. He used to remind friends that in his early life, part of his job entailed taking parties on exploratory trips into the deepest parts of the African continent. The groups were made up of geologists, archaeologists and other such experts, and on their trips they were usually accompanied by locals who carried all the necessary equipment.

From many years of hard experience, Rhodes knew that the faster he marched his mixed groups of experts into the interior, the more financially rewarding the results were likely to be. To keep up a rapid tempo, however, was more easily said than done. Despite his best efforts to maintain a 'forced march' pace and thus open up an opportunity to penetrate unexplored territory, he was often unsuccessful. Why? Well, after about four or five days of 'forced march' pace, he would awake one morning to a calamity. The professional experts in the group would be up and ready to depart. The locals would also have risen but – much to his chagrin – instead of having the packs and equipment on their backs, they would be sitting in silence on top of their bundles. As Rhodes told his story towards the end of his life, he explained that the leisurely habits of the locals might easily bankrupt him for he knew that if he could not smarten up the whole operation his customers would not reach unexplored territories and find profitable treasure. As he said, 'I personally would have been financially ruined and was so desperate that I had to take desperate measures. I first threatened to shoot every last native in the group if they did not take up the packages. When that failed to move them, I tried bribery and extra payments – but that didn't work either. Finally, one of the natives would bluntly explain the problem to me. "Sir," he would say, "we have travelled too far and too fast, and now we have to sit for a while and let our 'spirit' catch up with the rest of us."'

So it may be for you and me. We may also require similar moments of 'time out' and 'stillness' to allow our spirit to catch up with the rest of ourselves. Start with yourself by taking on some of the exercises below. In the space you create, try to notice how you are and how you have been during these past few months. Do not be too hard on yourself. That may be self-defeating. It's true that we are sinners but, hopefully, we are not hopeless cases and we do have the ability to change. You don't need to take a course in psychology to know this. Nor do you have to be a priest who spends long hours in the confessional to know that human nature has a tendency to concentrate on negative feelings such as self-condemnation and self-hatred. You may feel a little like G. K. Chesterton, who, when asked by the London *Times* to write an article about what was wrong with the world, wrote back, 'Dear Sirs, I am.' If you allow an air of depression to overwhelm you, it is likely that you will feel that none of your prayers will be answered, and, if so, you would be in good company. Remember Moses, who prayed that he might lead his Israelites into the Promised Land, or King David, who prayed that his infant son might be saved, or Job, Jonah and Elijah, who prayed that they might die quickly. None were successful in gaining what they asked for, at least not at the time they made their request or in the manner that they wanted their request attended to. Even Jesus himself, praying in the Garden of Gethsemane, asked that his future be changed and that the cup of bitterness might be removed from his lips. It was not. So the fact that our request might be turned down should not deter us from making our prayers of pleading and beseeching. The ancient Chinese had a saying: 'Be careful what you ask for. You might actually get it.' Remember that, in the Lord's eyes, our prayers may be untimely, inopportune or contrary to our own well-being. That may be the reason they are not being answered on this occasion.

So, try to remember a few simple guidelines. Ask clearly for what you want. Almost everybody I know says they are busier than they want to be and don't pray as much as they would wish. This is probably never going to change so, despite the pressures, carve out whatever time you can for prayer. The third hint or strategy during prayer might be to keep knocking even if a reply does not seem imminent.

Try to batter down the gates even if you are unsure whether you are being heard. We get that tip from Christ himself. Throughout the gospels he constantly praises people who won't take 'no' for an answer. Sometimes the response to our petition appears likely to be a negative one. In such cases we are advised to be careful what we ask for. The gods, we are told, when they wish to correct an unwise or foolish request, give supplicants exactly what they asked for. When it seems as if our request is receiving a negative response we might also bear in mind the gospel story of the woman who had to deal with an unjust judge. There, the initial 'no' turned out to be more of a 'we'll see', and the woman was praised for her persistence. Circumstances may change in any given situation and, as any wise parent will tell you, 'we'll see' leaves a lot more room for manoeuvre than a definite 'no'.

Pastor David Mains suggests that when we get down to prayers of petition, the following checklist might be helpful to us. Firstly, what do I really want? Am I being specific, or am I just rambling on about nothing in particular? Secondly, can God grant this request? Or is it against God's nature to do so? Thirdly, have I done my part? For example, am I praying to pass exams when I haven't attended class or studied for the subject I am taking? Fourthly, how is my relationship with God at the moment? Are we on speaking terms or have I spent any time with him lately? Will he even vaguely know where the request for assistance is coming from? Fifthly, who will get the credit if my request is granted? Am I at all likely to go back and acknowledge the source of my good fortune? Lastly, do I really want my prayer answered? What difference will it make?

Prayers of petition are one of the ways we pray, but we may do so to gain some perspective on how we are living our lives. In South Africa, Bishop Desmond Tutu says as much. He accepted the job of presiding over the Truth and Reconciliation Commission hearings there. Terrible stories of beatings, electric shock torture, rapes and the like could have plunged the country into total despair. A reporter asked Tutu how he kept a spirit of hope alive within himself and why he kept up his practice of prayer. He replied, 'If your day starts off wrong, it stays skewed.' He knew that he needed to take time out just to keep things in some kind of perspective. When the same bishop was asked by Bono, of the famed Irish music group, U2, how he managed to hold on to his faith and his practice of prayer amid the destruction and evil that surrounded him, Tutu replied, 'What are you talking about? Do you think we'd be able to do this stuff [the work towards reconciliation] if we didn't?'

Other reasons were supplied by a number of Irish Jesuits who were asked during a summer conference what prompted them to pray. What method or prayer style did they find most effective and what tips had they for what really helped? A number of their replies stood out for me. Many mentioned that if one commits to prayer one has to accept that for much of the time nothing seems to be happening. The process involves wasting time (or at least spending a fair amount of time in silence). Some pointed out that they prayed most regularly when they were in need and when they were afraid. One mentioned that some of his best prayer occurred when he thought he was dreaming because his prayers had a 'dream-like' quality about them. Others said that their prayer consisted of bringing to the Lord the issues and pressures they were currently facing. I myself have noticed that when I am in the middle of preparing for a talk, a workshop or a retreat, I am forced to reflect on what has been going on in my life, and that provides solid material, which needs to be chewed over in a reflective and prayerful manner. If I try to pray only for myself I am blank. The last two inputs that particularly struck me were one man's observation that 'prayer is trying to be faithful to my life, and not letting it become one damn thing after another. I have to savour its richness, feel its pain, acknowledge its tedium and celebrate its love. Prayer is most aptly described as letting God love me. He does. It is my job to notice, to remember and to relish.' Finally, one of the contributors said that praying, from his earliest years, had gone through four phases. 'First, I shouted at God. Then I shouted to him. After some time I tried to listen to God and now, during these last years, I try to make it my business to listen for God. Who knows what comes next?'

Before beginning this exercise it is often a good idea to find a suitable time in your day when you can be alone, quiet, and at peace. Many find that early in the day before distractions set in is a good time, or perhaps you might be happier choosing the late evening when your daily labours are finished.

Choose a suitable location – quiet and undisturbed. Allocate about twenty minutes for the exercise and hope to increase this to thirty or forty minutes as you get more used to the process.

Settle yourself in a seated position on a straight-backed chair and place your hands in your lap.

Close your eyes and relax.

Breathe in and out deeply and feel your whole upper body filling with air. Build up a gentle and rhythmic pace of breathing – this should help you to relax. Draw the air in through your nostrils and imagine it coming to the back of your mouth and entering your throat before coming down through your windpipe and towards your shoulder area. Allow it to then move slowly downwards through your arms and into your fingers. Imagine your chest area filling with air and notice the air circling around your backbone and then travelling down to the pit of your stomach. (If you place your hand over the centre of your stomach you should be able to feel it reaching the belly button spot).

As you breathe inwards and outwards, it may help to pace yourself if you count slowly and silently as you breathe in and out. Count slowly to four as you breathe in, and, after a short pause, count a further four beats as you breathe gently out. This should help you to slow down your breathing pattern and produce a heightened, mind-calming effect.

With your eyes closed, see if you can become aware of the sensations that present themselves. Notice the air as you breathe it in and out. Recognise the coolness of the air on each inward breath and the slightly warmer feeling as you breathe out through your mouth.

Keep up that quiet, gentle pattern of breathing in and out for a few minutes. When you feel suitably still and quiet, imagine Christ is sitting there beside you and just spend a few moments alone with him.

At first this whole process may be difficult. Any new activity takes time to master. Most of us have our minds bombarded with noise and confusion during the day and a certain amount of 'winding down' may be necessary before we begin. You need to relax and still your mind. When you feel ready, try to become aware of how you find yourself at the present moment.

After a few minutes, conclude the exercise.

Whenever you're ready, let's begin. With your eyes closed, you can begin to relax, though at first all sorts of distractions may come along and try to put you off your stroke.

Images or pictures drift into the mind automatically. It's hard to be still and remain in the present moment and sometimes it is even more difficult to allow your mind to begin to experience a gradual letting go.

Letting go may mean that you let go of how your legs are feeling, or whether the left leg is feeling heavier than the right ... just relax as the mind begins to drift down or even upwards towards that place of quietness and calm awareness ... a place of effortless relaxation ... just letting go...

Try to relax and let things happen, almost by themselves ... for this is your time.

You have a conscious mind and a subconscious mind that will keep you tuned in, even if it feels like you are falling into a deep sleep ... so just be aware of your body and how it feels now.

Start to become aware of the tiny muscles around your eyes and eyelids ... invite those muscles to begin to relax ... let that feeling begin to spread down into your cheeks and then down into your jaw, your ears, all around to the back of your head ...feel your own scalp now ... and then allow it to flow down into your forehead ... feel your worry lines relaxing and your face becoming relaxed ... now down to your neck ... down to your shoulders.

As you breathe, be aware of any sensations going on in your left shoulder, left arm, left wrist, into your hand, your fingers, and let your left arm begin to relax on its own as you move your attention to your right arm and go down the various parts as you did with the left ... note any differences between your left and right arms ... which feels lighter or heavier? Or are they both the same ?

Now become aware of the sensations in your upper back ... you may well have watched warm wax trickle down the side of a candle, so allow that feeling of relaxation to trickle down your back and spread down to the back muscles ... become aware of the relaxation taking place in your chest and then your stomach ... a nice feeling of relaxation in your tummy, and then down to your legs, your thighs and your feet.

As you inhale and exhale, send a wave of relaxation spreading down your whole body ... stay with the peace of that feeling ...

In your mind, count back from ten down to one and, as you count backwards through the numbers, try to observe yourself becoming more and more relaxed ... ten, becoming more relaxed, nine, arms becoming heavy, eight, deeper again, feel the weight of your body, seven ... deeper again, six, deeper still, five, four, three ... deeper still, two and one.

Deeper and deeper ... your whole being becoming drowsier... feel your whole body soaking up the nourishment of relaxation ... try not to slip over into sleep. When you are ready begin to settle yourself and gently begin to sketch a scene in your imagination.

Begin by settling yourself in a quiet place.

Take up a posture suitable for prayer – sitting, kneeling or lying down.

Use your breathing pattern to come to an inner stillness.

Now, in your imagination, picture yourself moving towards and into a temple or church. You require some moments of quiet. Notice the crowd in the church already gathered around the lectern. It's a midday service and the celebrant has handed a gospel text to one of the congregation. The text is one we know quite well and Jesus is the person who has been asked to do the reading. As he opens the text, he begins to speak.

The spirit of the Lord is upon me,
Because he has anointed me to preach good news to the poor.
He has sent me to proclaim freedom for the prisoners
And recovery of sight for the blind.
To release the oppressed ...

After the reading, Jesus closes the book and allows his eyes to rest on you. He slowly makes his way over towards you and together the two of you make your way to a quiet part of the building.

In your imagination, see Jesus telling you that the spirit of God may have been given to him, but it has also been offered to you. He tells you that you have been called or chosen, and that can be a bringer of the scriptures to liberate those around you.

Jesus then invites you to be a partner in his work, but first you may need to unburden yourself of your own troubles. He wonders which parts of your life are not free or which of your practices tend to cripple you.

He invites you to identify people whom you have shut off because you did not offer them forgiveness, and others you discounted by judging them too harshly.

He helps you to cast your mind back and think of people you did not value as you should.

Next Jesus encourages you to name fears or threatening individuals whom you allow to oppress you. Why does this happen? What can be done about it?

Now Jesus takes his leave of you so that you can quietly chew over what you have been discussing with him. As he departs, you begin to reflect on the areas of your life that keep you from being fully human and fully alive.

Might it be the area of relationships, authority, work?

Or is it the area of personal habits such as drink, drugs, sexuality or being over-bothered about your own reputation and how you are seen by others?

When reading the passage, I try to peruse it like a letter that God might send me, rather than as if it's just any book. I try to read slowly, pausing where necessary, allowing time for thoughts or revelations to sink in. I read in silence, trying to make the experience intimate and prayerful. As I finish the reading, I pick out any thought or feeling that struck me particularly. This thought becomes the bridge to the second phase of my prayer experience – the thinking phase.

2

WHY PRAY – AND WHERE MIGHT YOU START?

Silence is the atmosphere necessary to perceive God's presence.
Pope John Paul II

A colleague of mine recently came back from the United States having completed a month's course on spiritual direction. She was, I suspect, pretty good at praying even before she took the course, but she went to learn as much as she could about the subject. When she got back, I tried to pick her brains. 'The curriculum they made us go through,' she explained, 'was practical and very "hands on". What surprised me most, I suppose, was the source book our teachers had picked out for us before we began.' When I enquired what that book might be, she mentioned the Old Testament Book of Tobit. I was a bit nonplussed as I knew virtually nothing about the book in question. When I went to explore, I found that one of its central characters is an angel called Raphael. In the book, this angel declares that he has come to help Tobit and he mentions that he has not come of his own accord but has been sent by God. Tobit, the ministering angel feels, will be a tough nut to crack, but he has a job to do, and even though he knows it won't be easy, he intends to get on with the mission.

I'll break off at this point to confess that angels aren't normally very high on my agenda. I don't think about them much and honouring them or giving them a great deal of deference is far from my normal course of action. The course that my colleague had attended had run over the Christmas period and, in the Lectionary, one can hardly fail to notice the number of times angels crop up in the daily readings about that time. Angels play a major role when it comes to the story of Jesus – and how he introduced himself to the world. You have only to think of Joseph and Mary, or Simeon, or the father of John the Baptist, or even the Wise Men or the shepherds to see how angels dramatically altered their lives. All those mentioned above were visited by angels and guided by them.

During that same Christmas period I was due to give a retreat in England. As I sat down to prepare the material, angels and the part they play in our lives began to surface in my consciousness. When I began with the retreat group some days later, the subject of angels was at the forefront of my mind. I, along with the retreatants, questioned whether they existed and, if they did, where and how they operated. One participant was clearly fascinated by the whole subject and took me aside as the retreat progressed. She shared her story with me and I really liked it. It's a bit complicated but I think it's worth staying with.

The lady in question – let's call her Margaret – had a really good friend named Alison who lived close to her. The two confided on an almost daily basis. Some months ago Alison had to relocate to a new city as her mother had become seriously ill and needed to be looked after. Margaret mourned her departure and felt her friend's absence terribly. Not only had she no one to bounce ideas off but she worried that Alison might become depressed with the new responsibilities and worries she found herself faced with. For these reasons, Margaret decided to purchase a plaster angel as a gift for her friend. It wasn't easy. Models of angels were in short supply in her local shops but she did finally unearth one and sent it off. She told Alison that she was praying to both their guardian angels and putting their concerns completely in the angel's hands.

A month or so later the two ladies met up for a reunion. 'Did you get the angel I sent you?' Margaret asked. 'I did, and I got more than I bargained for,' Alison replied. 'I have to admit that around the time I received your angel I was scared and unsure of myself. Probably because of this I went to consult with a clairvoyant in my new town. I asked this woman if she could forecast what the future might hold for me. The poor lady did her best. For a couple of minutes, however, she looked closely at me in a confused sort of fashion and said nothing. Needless to say, I got more and more alarmed. I thought that she had seen some disaster looming for me. When I finally managed to get the clairvoyant to explain what the problem was she simply said that she was having difficulty getting her psychic powers to work. "I don't know how to explain this, but I normally read a person's future by looking at the auras around them. With you, all I can see is a protective angel sitting on your shoulder." ' By way of explanation, Margaret explained that she firmly believed ' that the angel she had sent had taken up this position and was doing a good job. Perhaps she's right. In this chapter we will try to find out if we too might have an angel sitting on our shoulders who can guide us in the ways of prayer.

To help us look at how we might deepen our inner life, it might be helpful to look at the prayer life of others and see if they have any useful hints about holiness and prayer. Mother Teresa used to say that to keep a lamp burning, you have to keep putting oil in it. Anthony de Mello was also very concerned about keeping alive our own inner spirit and offered suggestions about the same – he asked us to take time off regularly in order to see where we are finding fruit in our lives. Thomas Merton, too, recommended taking time out. He used to say that, for him, prayer was an expression of who he was. The late Cardinal Carlo Martini, the Italian Jesuit, explained things a little differently. He said that prayer time, for him, is really God's exertion and not ours. God speaks as softly as he can, and as loudly as he needs to. Our job is to listen. The more faithfully we listen to the voice within us, the more likely we are to catch sight of God. Henri Nouwen, another prayer guide who wrote well about the whole prayer process, said that when we pray we walk in the full light of God. In effect we are saying, 'I am human and you are God'. In *The Cloud of Unknowing*, a classic book of Christian mysticism from the fourteenth century, the process of prayer is described as an intense encounter with God who loves us passionately and who unites us with himself in a loving, illuminating, purifying, transforming and gratuitous way. It attempts to describe the space in which God and the human meet. It speaks about the 'cloud' or 'cloud of unknowing' within which one is united with God, and the author uses words like 'darkness' or 'the absence of knowledge' to describe this space. The book maintains that all prayer is a gift and we must wait patiently upon God for it.

Even though faith and grace are gifts, it seems likely that some effort on our part is necessary. St Ignatius of Loyola says as much. In his book of spiritual exercises he encourages those around him to find times of silence in their lives but explains that this may not be as easy as it seems. Forces outside our control are at work and we should never underestimate the possibility that as well as agents for good being active on our behalf, there may also be forces of evil lurking about. St Ignatius explains in some detail how he personally encountered both of these forces in his own life. At first he found it difficult enough to distinguish between the positive and negative 'spirits' which were directing his thoughts and actions. To help guide his footsteps, he devised a method – usually described as the 'discernment of spirits' – whereby he might be able to distinguish from which source the impetus for his actions was coming. He noted that both the 'good' and 'evil' spirits were capable of giving him feelings of great joy so how was he to distinguish between them? The secret, he found, was to carve out time after events had taken place to review the effects they had left behind. Events or happenings directed by the 'good' spirit' – when prayed about afterwards – increased the positive feeling within him, whereas those coming from the 'evil spirit' left him disconsolate. Those 'evil spirit' manifestations did not offer true and lasting consolation and were not to be trusted. Ignatius noted that in times of spiritual desolation we should be on our guard and hold off making decisions about our future. He stressed that it is usually wiser to wait for calmer times to arrive before deciding in which direction to proceed. This was echoed by St John of the Cross who, during his lifetime, went through many trials and tribulations that deepened his wisdom about prayer. Imprisoned for six months and scourged because he had tried to reform spiritual practices that had grown lax, he claimed that the reason most people do not reach close union with God is not because they are not called to such intimacy, but because they are unwilling to be purified. St Francis de Sales followed this thought and advised those who wish to pray to take time out to observe the spirits at work, and to beware of all brooding introspection. God's spirit will have difficulty dwelling in a soul if that soul is preoccupied with self-analysis. He suggested that one should 'jog along' as best one can in matters of prayer, and if you find yourself attacked by sadness or bitterness you should hand yourself over to the good spirit and try to relax in the Lord. He noted that some people seemed to lose hope when it came to prayer and gave up without really trying, while others expected God to come along with a magic wand while they sat back and did nothing. Neither course of action was satisfactory, but he did mention an option that might be worth looking at. If we look at the events of each day and try to see them as a form of disguise that God uses, we may be able to find God in those very events. By tuning ourselves more alertly into those events, we may be able to hear God's voice more clearly. This may be particularly true of bleak events which entail suffering. No one wants to encounter events such as these, but suffering is too precious to be wasted. As we see in the life of Our Lady, it was her willingness to stay with and ponder difficult situations that allowed her to hear God's word. It often seems that it was her courage in adverse conditions that gave her true greatness. At the foot of the cross, Mary was sensitive not only to her own pain but more especially to the pain and needs of others.

Praying in times of pain is not easy but can be profitable. This fact was brought home to me quite forcefully during my earliest days as a Jesuit novice. One of my fellow students was a youngster from a rural Irish background. He may have looked like a simple country boy with an extremely gentle nature but his mind was as sharp as a razor. His studies led him in psychoanalytical directions. In time, he learned to assist others to discover their own truth. He used to tell us that this truth often emerged through early and very painful memories. When we asked him how exactly he achieved his results, he explained in his own gentle fashion. 'I listen to those I work with – listen for the Word – because many people are isolated by anxiety. They are literally dying to be heard. Whenever I hear the unmistakable voice of the true self, as opposed to the echoes of coercive elders, I recognise in it the Word of God – but you have to be silent to hear.'

Most of us who lived with that student knew he had to work hard to develop his gift of listening. His own health was less than he would have liked, and at an early age he knew that he was likely to die much earlier than any of us might expect. Being a free spirit, learning through painful experience was not something that came naturally. A week before he died he recounted a dream that he had experienced. 'In the dream, I saw myself on top of a cliff and I had one foot planted solidly on firm soil. The other foot hung perilously out over a precipice. The only thing is that I don't know exactly where that other foot is going to land.' It takes courage to face the fear of not knowing precisely where the next step is going to lead.

Anthony de Mello was all too aware how fear of the unknown and fears about the future might stifle his listeners as they attempted to pray. When asked how he himself prayed, he said that when he was young he reminded himself that the Lord was present. Then he prepared two or three points and got to work. Beginning with the first point he went on praying, but often found himself getting distracted. When he mentioned this to an experienced guide, his tutor told him, 'You're not really praying at all – you're just thinking. Why not do something really simple? Imagine you are praying the Hail Mary and say something to Our Lady. Perhaps you might say "Holy Virgin of Virgins, pray for me". Keep it short. Keep it simple. That's prayer. Can you do that?' When de Mello replied that of course he could do that, he was asked, 'Then why don't you?' When he told us this story, he finished it with a short simple sentence. 'I never had much difficulty with prayer after that.' He explained that people have difficulty with prayer for a variety of reasons. They spend too much time thinking or they get distracted or they don't know what to do or haven't worked out exactly what they are praying for.

As we embark on our prayer journey, we begin – if we are alert – to see tracks or patterns. In the early stages we notice how uncontrolled our mind is. It resembles a puppy dog before training, running off in every direction at every whim. The mind has to be disciplined before the practice of meditation can bear fruit. When our mind wanders, we don't just allow it to go where it likes. Not if we desire results. We spring into action and restrain those distractions. There isn't much point in getting upset about them. Try to stay with the present moment. People meditate because they want to recapture a spark they felt they once had, to relax, to lessen some of their stress and to find peace of mind in their lives. As Christians, they also want to get in contact with their deepest selves and their God. Meister Eckhart, the German religious expert, said that there was really no such thing as a spiritual journey but that each of us in our lives needs to come into rhythm with our deeper natures. You don't have to go outside yourself to get into real conversation with your soul and the depth of the spiritual world. Listen to your core call. Think of God – not as an object outside – but rather as something intimate, an authentic encounter.

Another of my fellow students, when trying to explain why people prayed, said that he found a partial answer while pursuing one of his hobbies. As a youth, he used to keep racing pigeons in a loft at home. He was fascinated by them. Each week he entered them in competitions and had to transport them in boxes to some far-off location. They were homing birds and each had an identification tag. Many competing birds were dispatched from their home territory to this starting point for the race. The winner was the one who arrived home first. After you left your bird with a starter you dashed back to your home pigeon loft. You knew at what time the birds would be released and where they were being released from. The only thing you didn't know was when your bird was going to get back or if it was going to return at all. That's where the excitement lay. All the other owners had the same hopes as you. They believed that only a catastrophe would prevent their charge from getting home. They were sure that each bird possessed an instinct deep down that compelled it to return to base and that the bird would not be at ease until it reached home. My fellow student wondered whether we humans have a similar homing instinct that directs us back to God. To support his thinking, he quoted St Augustine: 'We were made for God and will not be happy until we rest in Thee'.

Anthony de Mello had many tips on how a prayer session might be conducted. He mentioned that on certain Indian retreats, the person conducting the prayer exercise begins by concentrating on an awareness of the breath pattern. Some prayer masters teach that breathing and being aware of the pace and rhythm of one's breath acts as a bridge from the known to the unknown.

In the quiet space that such observation provides, one notices a number of things. The mind seems to wander. It glides from events of the past towards dreams of the future and has difficulty – one might almost say an aversion to – staying in the present moment.

Observing the breath helps us to explore not only the reality of our bodies but also our minds. Material concealed in the unconscious rises to the conscious level and manifests itself in various physical or mental discomforts. It reveals something we may not have known – or more likely may not have wanted to admit to ourselves.

If you find it difficult to sit still during such exercises, the self-awareness and insights – sometimes painful – may let you know that you are getting close to important revelations. They may also let you know why it's hard to remain focused. Run through this checklist in your mind before you begin.

Have I chosen a relatively quiet room?
Is the time I have allocated sufficient?
Can I make it a regular time slot in my day?

Try not to eat immediately before meditation as a full stomach is not conducive to calm and peace.

You may well find that subdued lighting in the prayer space is helpful.

A good posture, aided by a comfortable seat or prayer stool, is likely to be beneficial.

Try to avoid distractions and minimise obvious sources of disturbance such as noisy doorbells or mobile phones.

Take your home phone off the hook.

If young children are around, try to get somebody else to look after them while you are at prayer.

If, during meditation, you realise that your mind has drifted gently off the subject matter you are working on, quietly notice that fact and bring your attention back to where you need it to be.

Do not finish your meditation too abruptly as your body is likely to be in a relaxed state – emerging from that tranquil environment too quickly leaves an unpleasant aftertaste.

Where possible, finish your meditation with the Lord's Prayer.

'One Sabbath day Jesus was teaching in one of the synagogues, and a woman was there who for eighteen years had been possessed by a spirit that left her enfeebled; she was bent double and quite unable to stand upright. When Jesus saw her, he called her over and said, "Woman, you are rid of your infirmity", and he laid his hands on her. And at once she straightened up, and she glorified God.'

When making use of a gospel passage during prayer know that you are going to read the Word of God in order to listen to what God has to say to you. Prepare yourself by asking God to send his Spirit with enlightenment. Without that, it is impossible to receive the Word or discover what message God is offering today. As the Carmelites say, you must build your cell within and around your being. So ask yourself, what is the text trying to say to me? Enter into dialogue with the text.

Go to that scene in your mind.
Put yourself in the woman's place.
Think of her bent double, a crone doubled up over her stick.
She is unable to see anything ahead of her – only the little vista around her feet.
She sees just the little patch she will shortly be stepping into.
Clearly her view is very restricted.
How have I been like that?
What have I not seen? Refused to see? Been unable to see?
When Jesus saw her he called her over.

He not only gave her relief from her physical pain but also a new way of looking at things.

The ability to take a much broader view of what was going on around her.

Has Jesus also called out to me?

Has he offered me new ways of looking at the world?

If so ... where/when/through whom?

What do I risk by looking up?

Try to discover what the text is saying to you.

Are any sentences jumping out to you?

Do any responses spring to mind? Is there anything you want to say to the Lord?

Check what you read in the Bible and how it matches what is going on around you.

Try to find out what the living Word, which God is speaking to you today through the passage, is all about.

Continue to mull over what struck you most as you read the passage.

Why do you think that thought struck you so forcibly?

Speak to God about what struck you.

Listen to God's response.

It's hard to know how God might respond, but if you sit with an open mind and an open heart, perhaps an image will come into your mind, or a memory of what someone has said to you recently. The implications of a recent experience of yours may come into focus. End the meditation by praying the Lord's Prayer slowly.

When reading the gospel, don't read it like a book but treat it rather as a letter that God might have sent you.

Read it slowly, pausing when necessary and allowing time for the thought or message to sink in. Read quietly, trying to make the experience intimate and prayerful. As you finish, pick out a thought or feeling that struck you as you read. Try to make this become a bridge to the second phase of your prayer experience – the thinking phase.

Hearing something read, or hearing something read aloud by someone else, heightens your appreciation of it. It may also assist your mind to understand and remember the ideas presented.

The thinking phase of prayer is modelled by Our Lady when she pondered deeply the words that the angel Gabriel had spoken to her. During the thinking phase, one reflects about what one has just read. We've had the experience, as it were, and now we're looking for the meaning.

During the segment on the speaking phase of prayer, you might be helped by imagining Jesus as a companion walking by your side or sitting close by. Try to think of how two close friends might feel at ease when they are close to one another and model the relationship between yourself and Jesus in that manner. Anthony de Mello used to tell of a sick patient who found prayer quite difficult most of the time. He was told to place an empty chair close to his sickbed and imagine Jesus sitting in that chair. Now he had an image to cling to, and as soon as he started to paint such a picture in his imagination he found he no longer had huge difficulty communicating with God.

To get yourself started, choose a place that seems to you to be suitable for prayer, somewhere you can be alone and undisturbed, and without undue distractions.

Allocate a designated time period. Many books suggest that you choose a regular time each day so that your mind and body are somewhat prepared for the experience. However, do not let the absence of such a time hinder you.

Silence is generally a great help but if you are not used to being by yourself, or find the stillness a little threatening, you can use meditative music as a sort of backdrop. At the back of this book you will find a list of music that I sometimes use and find helpful. Many groups I work with have said that the music somehow helps to settle them and keep them focused to the task at hand.

In a similar way, you may find it helpful to light a candle before you begin your prayer as this lends an atmosphere of devotion to the occasion.

Finally, you may like to sit, kneel, stand or lie down to create a sense of tranquillity within your body. Keep your back straight and slowly close your eyes. Begin to observe your breath, which has its own particular pace and pattern. Without trying to change the pace, build up a good, steady rhythm. Do this by silently counting to four on each inbreath and again on each outbreath. Keep the tempo slow and regular. You might keep this up for two or three minutes until you have established a pattern. If your mind wanders, simply return to the process of observing your breath.

When you feel your body and inner spirit have settled down, let your imagination take over. Try to imagine you are in Lourdes, the holy venue in France. You may know the place from personal visits and, if not, just conjure up a representation of what you imagine the grotto looks like. Place yourself there with the child, Bernadette. Recall Bernadette's story, remembering that she was a poor child from a peasant family. One day, while out collecting firewood, she suddenly noticed a woman clothed in white standing nearby. The woman, in Bernadette's words, looked 'other-worldly', and, when asked, explained that she was the 'Immaculate Virgin'.

Now, still using your mind's eye, I want you to imagine that you are having an experience like Bernadette. See the Immaculate Virgin Mary, Mother of God, as she suddenly appears before you. Try to picture her revealing her story. Listen as she tells you about her newborn child. He was her son, her very own baby, and at the same time, he was also her God. In her own words, 'He is God, and yet like me'.

No other human person has experienced God like this. A God they can take in their arms. A God they can cover with kisses. A deity they can see and touch and communicate with here and now.

As Our Lady spoke simply and plainly to Bernadette, she might be equally generous with us if we ask. So ask. Being a mother, she was able to communicate easily and generously with her Son. Perhaps, if we ask her, she will teach us to do the same.

Find a quiet spot and settle down. When the activity in your mind begins to diminish, put together the following scene in your imagination. You are a tree. What type of tree are you? Are you big or small, bushy or scraggy, tall or short, grand or rather plain?

Now note where you have been planted. Are you in rich soil that nourishes you or in a barren landscape? Do you exist on your own, or are there other trees in close proximity?

If other trees are present around you, are they of your type or a different variety? Do you live your life quietly in isolation or do you regularly discuss how things are going with those around you?

When you feel ready, allow your attention to focus on your roots. How healthy are they? Is the soil they find themselves in sustaining and nutritious? What exactly keeps them healthy? Do they feel deprived in any way?

As a tree you live through different seasons.

Imagine yourself first in the season of autumn. Feel your leaves changing colour and drying up. Something is stirring within you, so get in touch with this approaching feeling of dryness in your leaves and branches. As your covering begins to fall away, how does that affect the way you feel?

Now the seasons begin to revolve. Autumn gives way to winter and the seasonal chills rip off the last of your leaves. What's it like for you now that you are completely exposed to the elements? It's true that the chills of winter have decimated the lushness that previously supported you, but perhaps they have done you a good turn as well. In the balmy conditions, insects and other nuisances may have taken up residence within or around you. Some of the unhealthy baggage that clung to you during more affluent times may now be burnt away in these more primitive circumstances.

Nothing lasts for ever. The starkness and brutality of winter begins to soften and the first signs of new life start to appear. Notice the ice beginning to loosen and melt and the first signs of fresh water start to reach your roots. Hints of warmth start to touch your core and the gentle climate encourages new growth. See and feel fresh buds within you growing and bursting into life. Try to notice what is growing within you and which parts of you are changing.

Now move on to summer. Conditions are right to encourage maximum growth. How are you responding to these conditions? Can you do anything special to facilitate new growth?

Now take a few moments to become a person again and be present as yourself here in the room. Try to get in touch with the experience you have just been through and see what similarities there are between your life as a tree and your daily life as a human being. Would you like to change something in you or in the tree?

Take a few moments and, when you are ready, end the exercise.

3

USING YOUR BIRTHRIGHT

The boat is safest when it is in port, but that is not what boats were built for.
Paulo Coelho

If you happen to like storytelling, as I do, you'll know a good tale when you hear one. This was the case recently when my attention was caught by an anecdote shared among walking companions. As we strolled along, one of the gang suddenly began to relate how a relative of hers seemed to have lost her mind. The form of her madness was unusual. She was giving away fifty-euro notes to anyone who asked for them. That sounded interesting and most of the walking group tuned in to the story straight away, for they all agreed that there had to be a catch in the tale somewhere. As our raconteur picked up on our interest, she lightened the atmosphere by adding in a humorous voice, 'You may be surprised to hear that I've been visiting that same relative myself rather a lot lately.'

So who was this relative and why was she giving money away? It took some time to winkle the secret out of her but it transpired that the lady in question was an honest farmer's wife who had enjoyed a pretty good life. For years she had been satisfied with her lot and never neglected to count her blessings. It seems she had a good marriage, her health was in decent shape too, and – while money was not exactly flowing out of her pockets – neither was she in any great want. She was fairly normal, then, but what was unusual about her was that she went to bed one night feeling that all in the world was well with her and that God was good ... and woke up the next morning only to find that she had won a fortune in the Irish National Lottery.

No doubt, like me, you are thinking that all her ships had come in at the same time. 'Some people have all the luck,' you may say. But that's not how the lucky woman herself viewed things. She had won the Lotto right enough, but instead of asking herself the usual question that you or I might have stumbled on, 'What do I want that I do not already have?', she wondered if there was anything that she really needed that she was now doing without. To her surprise, she discovered the answer was 'nothing'. In fact she felt that her new-found wealth might, if she was not extremely careful, upset her equilibrium in life.

It was then that she hit upon the idea of spreading her good fortune among those who asked for it. News of her generosity raced around her area. Neighbours and relatives came from far and wide. When last I heard, half the country seemed to be beating a path to her door. No one was disappointed and not a single person who came to her house left empty-handed. Everyone got a little – though whether it did them any good or not I am unable to say.

As our fellow-walker finished the story, she said that the lady had not only won a million but was herself one in a million. Not many people, as far as I can see, are awake enough to notice what gifts and strengths they have been given. Neither are they truly aware of their blessings while they still have them. The Irish writer Nuala O'Faolain expressed this same thought beautifully a while ago when she discovered she had a terminal illness and was shortly to die. 'As soon as I knew that I was going to die, the goodness went out of life', she said. In an Irish radio interview she remarked that when she became aware of her imminent death, it amazed her how quickly life turned sour. 'For example, I live somewhere beautiful, but it means nothing to me any more, the beauty.' She never really valued her health properly until she was in imminent danger of losing it. Others have observed something similar. They say they don't notice gifts they possess until they are about to lose them. It may well be the same for us. We have all been given some sort of birthright, but have we noticed or used it? Do we even realise that it is there at all? So my first point about 'birthright' is a request that we notice that it is present – both to and for us.

My second request is that we do not take what we have been given for granted. This point came home rather forcefully to me recently when one of the lecturers at the university where I work died unexpectedly. He was a lovely character with a really generous heart that always seemed to notice the needs of those around him. This gift meant that he often seemed to gather around him marginalised types such as orphans or immigrants. Their common characteristic was that they all seemed to be down on their luck, so he let them stay in his house for weeks or months on end. He himself was a Protestant but many of those he helped were Catholic and if their problems had a faith edge to them I was often invited over to his house to see what I could do. So, when he died suddenly, his widow phoned me and asked if I would like to give the sermon at his funeral. Of course I would. As the service would be held in the local Protestant church I was not sure about the correct procedure for speaking at the funeral. The local vicar solved my problem. He phoned and extended an invitation to his church. When I arrived, the church was packed. As it was a Protestant church, I did not know many of those in attendance, but I did not really expect that would bother me or knock me out of my stride. Before long, I was proved wrong.

As soon as I got up to speak, trouble began. Jumping into action, I explained that I had three clear images of the deceased in my mind that I wanted to get across. Firstly, as he was less than conventional, I saw him fondly as an ageing hippie. Just thinking about him made me smile. He radiated effortlessness and was not concerned by the expectations of the world. Even his appearance – for he often wore open-toed sandals – had something of the hippy about it.

Next, I moved on to my second image and this one was taken from J. D. Salinger's book, *The Catcher in the Rye*. If you're familiar with the text, you'll remember that the central character, Holden

Caulfield, when asked what he wanted to do with his life, displayed a sort of messianic complex. He said that, in his imagination, he carried around a story in his head. In this narrative, he pictured himself in a field of tall rye or wheat. Loads of little kids ran around that field enjoying themselves. What they didn't realise was that the meadow they were in had a sheer cliff at the end of it and the kids were in great danger of falling over this precipice as it was hidden from their view. The hero of the book says that what he wanted to do with his life was to stand at the very edge of the cliff with his arms outstretched and save any kids before they fell over. He wanted to be the 'catcher in the rye', and that was exactly how I pictured our lecturer in my second image.

My third and final image was meant to complete the sermon. It was supposed to concentrate on the generosity with which our lecturer had used his gifts. He was brilliant at fixing things, and if you asked him for any assistance with computers or the like, not only was it given without delay but you actually felt that you yourself had played a large part in solving your problem. Just as I started to present this third image, however, my mind went completely blank. When I say blank, I mean blank. My third point had been very clear to me when I prepared the sermon but now it was completely gone and I hadn't the remotest idea if it was ever likely to come back. Thank goodness this happens very, very infrequently to me and you wouldn't wish the sensation to descend upon your worst enemy. Whenever it has happened in the past, I have always been able to throw the story back to the audience and ask them what they think might be likely to happen next. The few seconds gained by this tactic have always been enough for me to regain my composure and remember where the narrative should be leading. Not on this occasion. The congregation may not have realised it, but I knew that I was in big trouble. Nothing was coming. I had to be honest and tell the listeners that my third image had done a runner – and might never return. There was, I added, a positive side to this scenario. The sermon they were listening to would be shorter than expected, bearing out the saying that every cloud has a silver lining. With that, I sat down. As soon as I regained my seat, the missing third point came back to me instantly. When it did, I had the brass neck to ask the vicar if I could put the finishing touches to my presentation and supply the third point later in the service. He kindly agreed.

As I drove back home I began to reflect on whether or not God might have been speaking to me through the incident. Was he saying something about gifts and using them? It struck me quite forcefully that he may have been saying, 'My son, you are lucky enough to be able to preach and engage in public speaking without much effort. It comes easily to you. You think this is a bequest you will always have. It might be a wise move on your part to acknowledge that the ability to speak in public is in large part a gift. You may not always have it. Be a little less cavalier about this particular skill in the future. Be grateful for it now, and join in the prayer of Juliana of Norwich when she said of her gifts, "How lucky I am, how grateful I am".'

So my third recommendation is that you do not put the gifts you have been given on the back burner, because if you do they may well go away. Gifts or talents that are not used tend to die. This was highlighted for me last year from an unusual source when we got a request at our university. A musical group from an African school was touring England and Ireland and their benefactor – a distinguished British lady – was in a bit of a panic. She knew the orchestra was hard up for cash and one of their fund-raising engagements had fallen through. She wondered if they might put on an extra performance on our campus and, during it, make a collection to boost their funds. We agreed. During their presentation, one individual in particular stood out. He was older and smaller than the rest and stood with a crude-looking guitar at the back of the stage. He was, in fact, their lead guitarist, but was a most unlikely choice for that position. During the interval, the orchestra's benefactor asked him to step forward and tell his story. With some reluctance he did.

His start as a musician was unusual to say the least. He explained that he was the youngest in his Ugandan family and was so sickly at birth that no one gave him any chance of survival. His father despaired of his surviving at all and said that his poor mother had gone to all that trouble with very little to show for it. The father thus gave him a most unusual name. When translated, it came out as something like 'Born for Nothing'. With a start like that, the guitarist said shyly, your fortunes can only go upwards. Around the age of ten, the lad tried to get a job minding the local teacher's cows. It was about the only talent he had. He was very disappointed when no money was available for that job but surprised when the master said that if he was prepared to mind the cattle for nothing he could take school lessons for free. That's what he did and the whole experience was a nightmare. At least it was at first. He was older than the other boys and slower at picking things up. The lads laughed at his clumsy efforts. The only bright spot in his day was his cattle minding. One day, however, while on this duty, he came across the stump of a tree that had been damaged by lightning. He managed to hack the misshapen wood out of the ground and drag it back to school. In woodwork class, the master suggested making a guitar out of the charred remains and helped him create an instrument from the blackened material. That was his beginning. First he learned to pluck one string, then a chord, then a whole series of notes that produced a song. He even discovered he had a talent for singing and believed it could be developed if he was prepared to work at it and this he did constantly. He knew that if he let this spark of talent lie dormant, it would quickly fade. This, he was determined, would not happen and it did not. His presence on stage this evening proved that and now he proudly held up the blackened hunk of wood that he had made into an instrument. The guitar was black and charred but still somehow beautiful. The making of that instrument was the start of his redemption and after a time he got into the school orchestra. Now he was well on his way to becoming a real musician who could even make a living from his skill. He finished by telling us that he had changed his name to 'Born for Better'.

Many of us – if we pause for a minute – know that, just like that African musician, we were born for something better. We have talents, even if modesty or diffidence makes us slow to admit it. When pushed, we can come up with skills and attributes that emerged slowly within us. These skills may be a surprise to us, and possibly a surprise to others as well. Think for a moment. What are your particular gifts? Where did you get them? How best are you going to keep them and even increase their effectiveness? It may dawn on you that talents, if left unused, don't get any better. In fact, they probably begin to rust. It's a question of 'use them or lose them'. We may not always grasp this while thinking about our own life history. The stories of others can drive home the point.

In my own case, I only have to go back to my schooldays. One of my classmates was considered a hopeless case. Nothing seemed to come easily to him. For the first three or four years in class he seemed anonymous, and if you asked me in what way he stood out I would have nothing to say. Exam results came in and he made bottom place. The same was true for sports. He never looked remotely interested. You might say his train had hit the buffers, but that would be an exaggeration because his train had never really left the station. Then something dramatic happened. Great transformations sometimes have small beginnings and that was certainly the case here.

In our fourth year debating was introduced into our school. I think that was the catalyst for him. It was as if a seed long buried suddenly received water and light. This introverted youth – for so long unloved and unnoticed – burst into life. He somehow plucked up the courage to volunteer as a speaker in our first debate. He had found something he was interested in. That led to him putting in some preparation for the speaking event and, as he began to stir himself, he got involved in the goings-on around him. The results were amazing, for from that gentle beginning, his confidence grew and, as the Chinese philosopher Confucius has said that we learn wisdom through three channels; first by reflection, which is the noblest, then by imitation, which is the easiest, and finally by experience, which is the bitterest. So it was with my underachieving classmate. For years his whole being had lain dormant, his talents unrecognised. Now, at that first debate, he spoke. He wasn't brilliant – I'm not sure if he was even adequate – but the very fact that he spoke at all was a source of wonder to his mates. The little skill he was displaying was attracting interest from those around him. That spark of attention was enough to whet his appetite. He had somehow stumbled upon his own gift or birthright and, from hesitant beginnings, his talent grew week by week. Kind words encouraged him. He put his name forward again the following week and, when his more diffident classmates held back, he was given another opportunity.

Practice makes perfect, they say, and in this case it did, or at least the compliments and admiration he received were enough to fan the flames of his enthusiastic effort. The results were spectacular. All aspects of his life began to benefit. Success built upon success. Within two years, he was the star debater in the school. He worked for everything he got and, to the best of my knowledge, he has never looked back. The self-confidence he gained has stood him in good stead in other areas of his life as well. Perhaps you too can discover where your hidden talents lie and develop them with the same application?

Before beginning this exercise it is often a good idea to find a suitable time in your day when you can be alone, quiet and at peace. Many people find that a good time is early in the day before distractions set in, or perhaps you might be happier choosing the late evening when the labours of the day are finished.

Next choose a suitable location – quiet and undisturbed. Allocate about twenty minutes for the exercise and hope to increase this time to thirty or forty minutes as you get more used to the process.

Settle yourself in a seated position on a straight-backed chair and place your hands in your lap.

Close your eyes and relax.

Breathe in and out deeply and feel your whole upper body filling with air. Build up a gentle and rhythmic pace of breathing to help you to relax. Draw the air in through the nostrils and imagine it coming to the back of your mouth and hitting the back of your throat before coming down through your windpipe and towards your shoulder area. Allow it to then move slowly downwards through your arms and into your fingers. Imagine your chest area filling with air and notice the air then making its way downwards – circling around your backbone, then down to the pit of your stomach. (If you place your hand over the centre of your stomach you should be able to feel it reaching your belly button).

As you breathe inwards and outwards, it may help to pace yourself if you count slowly and silently as you breathe in and out. Count slowly to four as you breathe in, and, after a short pause, count for a further four beats as you gently breathe out. This should help you to slow down your breathing and produce a heightened, mind-calming effect.

With your eyes closed, see if you can become aware of the sensations that present themselves. Notice the air as you breathe in and out. Recognise the coolness of this substance on each inward breath and the slightly warmer sensation as you breathe out through your mouth.

Keep up that quiet, gentle pattern of breathing for a few minutes. When you feel suitably still and quiet, imagine Christ is sitting there beside you and just spend a few moments alone with him.

At first this whole process may be difficult. Any new activity takes time to master. Most of us have our minds bombarded with noise and confusion during the day and a certain amount of 'winding down' may be necessary before we begin. That's why you seek a time and place of silence, for you need to relax and still the mind. 'If God is to speak, then we must remain silent.' When you feel ready, try to become aware of how you find yourself at the present moment.

After a few minutes, conclude the exercise.

Sometimes an experience or incident from your own life can kick-start you into prayer. Let me give you an example.

Last year, I was wandering around the art museum in Munich when a large painting caught my attention. It was by Albrecht Dürer and I remembered hearing how he and his brother William had both been very promising and keen art students. The two of them hoped to continue in life as artists but knew that their family was poor and their chances of doing so were slim. At this point they came to an agreement and decided to toss a coin to determine their future. Whoever lost would go to work down the local mine, and for the next few years would support both the family and the lucky brother through art school. When the winner completed his studies, it was hoped that the money made through his artistic endeavours would be enough to allow the remaining brother to quit the mines and take up an artist's life as well. Albrecht won, William lost, and the elder brother began his art studies shortly afterwards. Before long, it became obvious that he had a rare talent, particularly in wood-cutting, and this became his speciality.

Some years later, as the art course came to its conclusion, Albrecht met with his brother to let him know that their original plan was going to work. His skill was such that he was getting paid commissions on a regular basis and these would enable the whole family to survive financially. William could now leave the mine and begin to pursue his artistic leanings. In reply, the younger brother simply clasped his hands together and held them up in the air. His gesture conveyed more information than any words could have done. It was obvious from a quick glance at his hands that no artist's work would ever be produced by them in the future, for over the few short years of heavy mine work they had become mangled and coarse and would not now be fit for the refined skills required of an artist. The younger boy had sacrificed his future so that his brother could fulfil his potential. When Albrecht was asked some years later to talk a little about his most famous creative piece, he said simply that he had produced it as a tribute to his brother. You will, I am sure, have seen representations of the work, known simply as *The Praying Hands*.

Using that story as a base point, find a quiet spot and work your way through the prayer exercise on the next page. First look down at your hands and think about the life they have gone through for a few minutes. When you feel ready, close your eyes and consider the following points.

(It might help if you record yourself speaking this meditation and allow it to play in the background so that you are not distracted by having to read the various segments.)

EXERCISE THREE: A PRAYING HANDS MEDITATION (THE GERMAN
DÜRER BROTHERS)

Recall the image you have just been looking at – your own hands. Imagine these hands as they were when you were a child, just forming, with so many potential gifts. Can you recall the first memory you have of using your hands? Were they used in a positive fashion or for destruction?

Move on to your youth and what your hands did for you during that period. You may have grasped opportunities or let them slip through your fingers. You may have been dexterous or butterfingered, tightfisted or heavy-handed, light of touch, or even light-fingered. How did you make use of the gift of your hands during your youth?

Remember the story of how these hands have operated. They may have clutched at straws or handled difficult situations firmly. In social situations, they may have held back, or stretched out towards strangers.

In their life, have they been gentle or cruel, hard or soft? They had the ability to feel and touch – how well have you used that ability?

Think of times when others needed your hands in their moments of pain or distress – to bless, comfort or hold them. How well did they do? Forgive them for when they were less than perfect.

Now cast your mind towards the future. Think of those who will need the gifts your hands have to offer. Make a prayer asking that the hands you see before you may be equal to the tasks put before them.

When you are ready, change focus slightly and move your attention to the hands of others. Whose do you remember? Go back to your childhood. How needy were you at that stage? Did others have to do virtually everything for you? Call to mind those who took on the bulk of your caring and call down a blessing on them. Conjure up images of those who cared for you in moments of need and place their intentions before the Lord.

Think ahead to the future and imagine times of sickness or old age (your sickness or old age). You will probably be reluctant to dwell on this image but do your best.

Send a blessing on ahead of you to rest on those who will give their time and gifts to attend to you and your needs when you reach that stage in your life.

EXERCISE FOUR: A MEDITATION ON ALBRECHT AND WILLIAM DÜRER (ALTERNATIVE VERSION)

Think about your hands and pray a prayer of thanks for them.

As you look down at your hands, observe whether they are open or closed.

Open hands are able to give and receive.

Ask that you may hold yours open.

Recall the times you were unable to keep these hands open ... the times you closed your fists in anger ... ready to fight ... or tightened them as you clutched at straws.

Hands in pockets show you don't want to show your hand. Have you often been reluctant to show your hand to others?

Clasped hands behind the back say 'no one is going to lead me on', so you pray not to have an inclination towards isolation or an inability to touch.

Clasped hands in front of the body often indicate a tendency towards self-protection. 'Help my trust, Lord, so that I remain approachable to others.'

Big hands may go with a big heart or big plans. Think of those who represented big ideas and pray that you may learn something from them.

Small hands show an eye for detail ... have you been able to see the bigger picture without losing sight of the finer details?

Hands holding each other create a continuous circuit, and allow each of us to pray for the other. Think for a few moments about those around you who may need your prayers.

Think of your fingers ... these have the ability to feel and touch. The fingers have extreme sensitivity – touch picks up information as well as leaving an impression behind.

Touch can give us pleasure but it can equally alert us to danger. Let your touch radiate warmth.

We let things slip through our fingers or hold on too long. Let your timing be right when you are involved in dealings with others.

We can be tight-fisted, open-handed, penny-pinching, butterfingered or handy. Let yourself be the last of those.

We give handouts, we can handle ourselves, or we can't seem to handle anything.

It's hands down, or hands off or out of hand, underhanded or open-handed. We have helping hands.

Hands can be gentle, or they can be hard.

Grasping hands come from fear, fear of loss, fear of never having enough, fear that it won't stay if you hold lightly.

Spend the last few minutes asking that your hands may be guided in the future; that they may be open to the possibilities before them; that they may be the hands of God in the world.

'Now this is how the birth of Jesus Christ came about. When his mother Mary was betrothed to Joseph, but before they lived together, she was found to be with child through the Holy Spirit. Joseph her husband, since he was a righteous man, yet unwilling to expose her to shame, decided to divorce her quietly. Such was his intention when, behold, the angel of the Lord appeared to him in a dream and said, "Joseph, son of David, do not be afraid to take Mary your wife into your home. For it is through the Holy Spirit that this child has been conceived in her."'

Read the meditation carefully.

Think about what struck you most as you read.

Why do you think you were struck by that particular point?

Speak to God about what struck you.

Listen to God's response.

It's hard to know how God might respond ... so be patient.

Sit with an open mind and an open heart and perhaps an image will come.

It might be a memory of what someone has said to you recently.

A recent experience of yours might take on new meaning or come into focus in a new way.

Finish the meditation with the Lord's Prayer.

Phase One: Reading

As you read the passage above, don't read it like a book.

Rather treat it as a letter that God might have sent you.

Read it slowly, pausing when necessary.

Allow time for thoughts or a message to sink in.

Read quietly, trying to make the experience intimate and prayerful.

As you finish the reading, pick out a thought or feeling that struck you as you read. This becomes the bridge to the second phase – the thinking phase.

Phase Two: Listening

Hearing something read out loud by someone else heightens your appreciation of it. This may assist your mind to understand and remember the ideas presented.

Phase Three: Pondering

This practice was modelled by Our Lady when she mulled over the words spoken by the angel Gabriel. You stay with the words or the image, trying to fathom what they might mean. You've had the experience, now you're looking for what it might mean.

Phase Four: Speaking

Anthony de Mello used to tell of a sick patient who found prayer quite difficult. A friend advised him to place an empty chair close to his sickbed and imagine Jesus or Our Lady sitting beside him. 'Just talk to them about the things going on in your life and what is bothering you', he would say. De Mello finished by saying with a smile that the guy didn't have too much trouble with prayer after that. Try it yourself and see how it goes for you.

4

LOOKING AT SITUATIONS IN A NEW WAY

You never have to change what you see, only the way you see it.
Thaddeus Golas

Changing your point of view is never easy. At least, I don't think it is but it's a gift that Tony de Mello often tried to bestow upon those who attended his seminars. Exactly how difficult it is to try to see things in a new way came home to me recently when I was in the United States and went to see an excellent one-man play there. The subject of the play was Thurgood Marshall, the first African-American appointed to the Supreme Court. The theatrical production brought us through some of the major events in his life and gave a little taste of what African-Americans had to endure in the fairly recent past in the Deep South of the United States. That's what I thought the play was about, anyway, but what life was actually like for that section of the population is difficult for a white person to experience or comprehend. That point was clearly brought home to me almost as soon as the show ended. In the foyer I met a fellow attendee who happened to be one of the few black people present at the performance. He was old, wise and gentle, and when I told him how much the play had affected me he said, 'You're white, well off, and free. How could you expect to know how awful it was down there unless you lived in the South? It might also have helped if you were desperately poor, and black. I was all three.'

This message was driven home even more fully the following day when I was saying Mass for some elderly citizens in a retirement home. When I told them about the above incident, one black lady added to my education. 'I was there too,' she said, 'and lived with my large family in a poor part of town. Most of the people in our area were black but right beside us we did have an impoverished white family. "White trash" they were called by the better-off whites and they were nothing to write home about, I can tell you. During a normal week things were not too bad but weekends were a disaster. During those days, most of the older white folks went out drinking and their kids suffered terribly. They were left to fend for themselves and as they were fairly young they didn't make much of a fist of it. Cooking was one of their bigger problems. The kids hardly knew what the word cooking meant so some days they just didn't get fed at all.'

Clearly my enlightener felt that her white neighbours should have looked after their own problems, but her father had other ideas. He was black, but smart as fresh paint and noticed everything that was going on around him. He saw straight away that those white kids were more or less abandoned – and so he took them into his own place. As the lady explained, all weekend those same kids played and ate with her family. 'None of us minded, for, to tell you the truth, their presence meant that time flew as we played together and the atmosphere in our yard was magic. Come Sunday night the scene changed quickly because their parents would stagger back home, start looking for their children, and pretty soon those white kids would return to their own homes.

'The part that really stays with me, however, was the Monday mornings. We black kids had to walk to school but the white children were bussed to their separate school, even though it was only three or four miles away. A big yellow bus used to come along and only the whites were picked up. Everyone knew that Negroes could not climb aboard. The thing I can't forget is what happened during our trek to school on those Monday mornings. All of us black kids walked, and as the bus passed us by as we sweated and trudged along in the fierce heat those very same white kids whom we had hosted the night before opened their bus windows. Those at the rear of the bus looked down upon us and hollered out in front of all their mates, "Hey niggers, keep walking." The sting of that comment still hurts me. I was so disgusted that the very first time it occurred I went straight to my Dad and said that those white kids next door were never to be invited to our house again. I still remember the look on my father's face. He appeared to be really shocked – and a bit let down. He began to ask me some embarrassing questions and wondered aloud if I had a nice house and was well treated in it. I said I had – and was. Then he asked who I loved. "You, Daddy," I answered. When that answer didn't seem to be the one he wanted, I tried "Mammy", and then "My brothers and sisters", but none of those seemed to hit the mark either. Finally, my Dad simply said, "Honey, before any of that you've got to love yourself first. Without doing that, you're unlikely to love others." He mentioned that the unfortunate children we took in had nobody and no home to welcome them at weekends. "What you've got with those white kids is special and wonderful," he said. "Forget about their actions when they get on their Monday school bus. At that point they are in front of their own kind and very restricted in what they can do or show. They feel compelled to act big and put on a tough face. They're not allowed to be themselves and they don't see how things are with their best eyes.'"

Her father, she explained, was pointing out that things are often not as simple as they seem, and that if we could stand back a little from events we might find it advantageous and be able to view gifts and values we've received more objectively. We were given a birthright at conception just by being human, and another at our baptism, when our parents brought us to church to be christened. In today's world more and more of us are failing to recognise that these things are gifts in our lives and we are in danger of letting our inheritance fall by the wayside through lack of appreciation of its richness. We need to look at this legacy in a new way if it is to retain its value.

An experiment carried out in one of America's foremost universities may explain more clearly this notion of viewing situations through 'new eyes'. It's a little difficult to describe as the research involved was subtle, but if you can picture the scene you may find it illuminating. When the volunteers assembled, the participants were asked to sit in a large semi-circle and split into two groups, A and B, but they were given no information regarding the purpose of the experiment. Group B were asked to keep their eyes closed while group A were shown a picture of a very elderly woman of about eighty. Then the process was reversed and Group B were shown their picture while the members of Group A kept their eyes closed. This time the presenter offered a picture of a much younger woman, aged about twenty-four, and the viewers were asked to fix this image in their minds. Now came the most important part of the experiment. All were allowed to keep their eyes open and this time the complete group was shown a third picture. This image was a composite of the two images already shown and was a smart piece of work. It contained both the old and young woman blended together but by some clever visual trick it was very difficult for the onlookers to spot this and all were asked to say what age they thought the woman in that final picture might be. When those who had first viewed picture A were shown the new image they were sure the woman in this third picture was an old lady and mentioned that she must have been about eighty. The second half of the group began to fall around laughing. They thought their companions must be bonkers because all they could see was a young woman who looked about twenty-four. Both groups were now looking at the same picture but viewing the subject from completely different standpoints. Even when they were asked to look at the material in a fresh way they found it virtually impossible to do so. The experiment was designed to point out what bias does to each of us. It succeeded brilliantly. It showed that we can get locked in to looking at situations in a certain way. Once that happens, it's extremely difficult to change our mindset. If we once lose sight of the value of the faith gift we have been given, regaining a sense of appreciation of that bequest will be extremely difficult.

Let's pause here for a moment and try to look at how we might retain an appreciation of our faith inheritance in today's climate. That seems an important issue to me, for strong winds have been buffeting that faith foundation in recent times – certainly in Ireland. This came home to me recently when I heard about a really unusual personality who works with the Tampa Bay Rays, a baseball team based in the United States. Your knowledge of baseball may be sketchy, and what you know about the Tampa Bay Rays may be even sketchier. To tell you the truth I don't know too much about the team myself, but I can tell you that they have a truly amazing radio commentator who helps them with their work. He presents regular match reports of their games to the local population and is a bit of a legend. His name is Enrique Oliu and his unique feature is that he cannot see – he is blind. If you wonder how a person without sight can present such a commentary, you are not alone. It defies logic. If he cannot see, how can he explain what is going on? But perhaps he can see – just not in the way that we usually mean when we use that word. The man himself says that if you think sight and seeing are the same thing, you have a lot to learn. 'If sight is perception,' he says, 'I can see as much as the next person', but what he 'sees' – and the way he 'sees' it – is unique and may be helpful to us in our faith struggle. I think he's saying that to understand something fully, you sometimes have to look at where you are, and what you believe in, through a different lens.

It's this notion of looking at things differently while trying to discern their value that I want to move on to. Some individuals have a special genius in this regard and I've met one or two in my time. One such turned up some months ago at a prayer weekend I was conducting. Usually weekends such as this include a liturgy prepared by the retreat participants. We asked for volunteers and a goodly number stepped forward. Their task was to choose and prepare a suitable gospel passage and present it to the whole group. On the weekend in question, those preparing the liturgy selected the gospel story where the disciples had gone fishing all night but had caught nothing. As daybreak approached, Christ suddenly appeared among them and – on hearing that their nocturnal activities had reaped no dividends – suggested that they might cast their nets from the other side of the boat, a very unpromising location. He hinted that this might achieve better results.

The weekend liturgy preparation group was clearly composed of original thinkers and they decided to hold our Mass outside on the day in question – in the beautiful grounds of the retreat centre. This little spot was unusual as it contained two small ponds that ran side by side, separated by a minuscule bridge. When we got to the gospel section of the Mass, the presenters stood up and, as one of them related the story, the others threw a fishing net into one of the ponds. Moments later, they drew the net up. It was empty. They then flung the net into the second pool and this time it emerged filled with paper fish. The storytellers had cut out images of fish during their preparation time and had placed these strategically within the pond so that they could be collected during the second dip. When the net emerged, they proceeded to distribute these cut-outs among the onlookers. Each of us was allowed take a fish, and as we took them in our hands we noticed that each fish had a single word, such as 'hope', 'peace' or 'love', written on it. You were meant to take the word on your fish as your theme for the day.

As each of us claimed our fish, one particular group began to dissolve into laughter. That group had among its number a blind man who had shown himself to be a great character throughout the weekend. What was cracking the group up was that the fish that this man had pulled out of the net had the word 'sight' written on it. When the man was told what had happened, he quickly joined in the laughter. He then startled us by saying that the situation was not exactly as it seemed. Though he appeared to be blind, he claimed that he had a type of 'seeing' not generally recognised by the ordinary individual. It just took a different form from ours. In fact, his 'sight' revealed even more to him than ours did. Though his eyes were shuttered, he could sense or 'see' atmosphere and ambience all around. He could usually tell whether those around him were in a positive or negative mood. His lack of sight had heightened his other senses. He could pick up whether or not he was being accepted and whether his presence was proving an embarrassment or a delight to other group members. 'Situations like these remind me to notice and develop what I have been given,' he said. That's where his experience may help ours – for if we can change the way we look at things it should help us to be grateful for the gifts we ourselves have been given.

Trying to change the way we look at the situations we find ourselves in is not easy. We very easily become fixed in our responses. Life has taught us to react to problems in a certain way, but perhaps the situation we now find ourselves in is different from a previous occasion, or perhaps we ourselves have grown or matured since we encountered our last difficulty. One particular example I really like came from Anthony de Mello himself. He was a master raconteur and he managed to include a 'sting in the tail' or a piece of advice for us in most of his yarns. He tells how he once travelled by train in India and found himself in a compartment with a young boy of about twelve years of age who was accompanied by his father. During their journey, the door of the carriage was thrown open and the ticket inspector put in an appearance. I should explain that junior tickets are valid up to the age of twelve but after that an adult version is required. The inspector first demanded to see each person's voucher and when he was examining the boy's permit he began to make unpleasant remarks. He became loud and overbearing and suggested that the lad looked much older than the permitted age for the concession rate. His snide remarks about how 'mature' the boy looked went on for a few minutes until the father's reassurances finally won through. As soon as the inspector departed and closed the door behind him, the young lad began to remonstrate with his father. He complained that the train guard was a buffoon, was uncouth, and had given the family no respect. During this tirade the father stayed silent. After the storm had blown itself out the father, very quietly, mentioned that the two of them had to put up with the poor man's behaviour for only a few minutes. He finished by adding that the unfortunate fellow had to put up with himself all day long. The father was teaching his son that it's not necessary to have your whole day ruined through the ignorance or uncouthness of another. You have to try and train yourself to look at the situation in a new way.

In a somewhat similar fashion, if we make time to look back on our faith journey of the past year we may also notice patterns. God's plan for us may become a little more apparent. You may be able to think of incidents in your own life where this was the scenario. I recall an incident in Africa some years ago when a Jesuit priest with whom I was working wanted me to experience something of the local culture. He was extremely busy himself, but knew that a wedding feast was taking place in a distant village. Sensing an opportunity, he suggested that I take his motorbike and make my own way to the feast in order to experience the colour and music of the occasion for myself. He maintained that I would have no difficulty finding the celebration, for the path from our house to the couple's village was not too far. The route was sandy scrubland – no formal road existed – but a way was marked out by small white sticks. This enabled me to reach the village shortly before sunset and in good time for the wedding feast. As my colleague had promised, the event was well worth the trip. In fact the whole occasion was so engrossing that time slipped by unnoticed. When I finally looked at my watch many hours later, darkness had fallen. Finding my way back would not be so easy. However, I feared that my absence back home might cause worry, so I began the return journey knowing that I had only to follow the white sticks and all would be well. For a time, things went according to plan. Then suddenly, in the inky blackness, the motorbike stopped. In my enthusiasm to begin the journey, I had forgotten to fill up with petrol and now my supply had run out. All alone, in the middle of the African wilderness, panic set in.

I began to hear all sorts of noises, either real or imagined. I could hear lions and tigers – I have subsequently discovered there are no tigers in Africa – and I also noticed that the front light of the bike was losing light rapidly as the battery wore itself out. The rest of the night was a terror. I had to switch off the light to conserve power, and then, switching it on for a few moments, I picked out the next white stick along the route. Switching the light off to conserve energy, I made my way through a series of short dashes from white stick to white stick. As soon as I reached each stick, I would pause for a few moments, switch on the light for a second, pick out the next white stick and, after again turning off the light, make a dash for it. Sometimes I was lucky. At other times, having run too far, I realised that I must have missed my point of reference. I then had to turn around and retrace my steps by means of my cycle tracks and return to my last known reference point. Eventually, hopping from stick to stick, I managed to get back to my colleague's village as dawn began to break. Those last few hundred yards were uphill and provided a high vantage point where I could rest. Only then did I look back. In the half light, a quite discernible line had been drawn in the sand and as I took the time I could clearly make out the route I and the motorbike had taken. It was easy to see, in retrospect, the occasions when I had gone off the track.

St Ignatius, the founder of the Jesuits, advised his followers to make use of this practice in their prayer lives. He suggested they discern what was going on within them, and by this he meant they should take time out, look back at their lifestyles and take note of the fruits that had been gained over the previous months. This practice would help them decide upon the wisest ways forward in the future. We are bound to fail and fall at times, but our ability to rebound and get back up off our knees in order to move forward is what separates the sheep from the goats.

EXERCISE ONE: THE OPEN WINDOW MEDITATION

Make use of a fantasy meditation to help you open up a space within which God and you might interact.

Relax yourself with a few deep breaths, and settle your body comfortably.

Imagine a window, through which a fine vista stretches out before you.

Now imagine that you are actually in front of this window and looking through it. In your mind's eye, what do you see through that open window?

What is out there waiting for you to explore?

After a few moments, allow your thoughts to waft out through the open window and float outwards and upwards. What can you see?

Maybe the sea, or a wood or a forest, comes to mind, or you might find yourself being transported through deserts or plains. Let your thoughts float free. Let everything come and go in an easy flow.

Don't hang on to any thought, no matter how important it may seem.

Allow yourself be transported to a delightful place such as the countryside or the seaside and enjoy the process, and then float onwards.

Enjoy this freedom. What are your feelings?

After some time with this exercise, reflect on how you are feeling here and now.

Did the minutes in this space feel liberating for you? Does your body now feel light or heavy? If you did feel something, and have a sensation of your thoughts soaring outwards, try to bottle that experience so that you might make use of it during a future, more stressful time.

When you feel ready, imagine yourself stepping back into the room through the window and come back to this present time and place.

Take time to get yourself back into reality. Open your eyes and acquaint yourself with objects in the room. Take time over this. Re-orient yourself fully before you get up.

Guided Imagery

The aim of guided imagery is to create in your mind's eye a particular picture, one that has particular significance for you. All we are doing here is using our imagination to create 'pictures' within and this seems to be an almost universal ability in human beings. The experience is a little similar to that of daydreaming but it does have one difference. In daydreaming our wandering is completely free and uncontrolled whereas guided imagery is done with a definite purpose in mind – it is 'guided' by whatever our purpose or intention might be. The unconscious likes to communicate with the conscious self through pictures and images just as it does in dreams, and Anthony de Mello used this form of imagery on many occasions to bring prayer participants more closely in touch with their deepest selves and with God.

EXERCISE TWO: NICODEMUS (JN 3: 1–5)

Among the Pharisees there was a ruler named Nicodemus. He came to Jesus at night and said, 'Rabbi, we know that you have come from God to teach us, for no one can perform miraculous signs like yours unless God is with them.' Jesus replied, 'Truly I say to you, no one can see the Kingdom of God unless he is born again from above.' Nicodemus said, 'How can there be rebirth for a grown man? Who could go back to his mother's womb and be born again?' Jesus replied, 'Truly I say to you, unless one is born again of water and the spirit, he cannot enter the Kingdom of God. What is born of the flesh, is flesh and what is born of the spirit, is spirit. Because of this, do not be surprised when I say, you must be born again from above.'

As you start a meditation, it is useful to have some idea about what you are aiming at and what you are looking for.

Begin by sitting quietly for a minute or two. Relax and settle down.

Now turn your attention to your breath and feel the sensation of each inhalation and exhalation as they flow naturally in and out of your body. As you breathe in, count slowly and silently from one to four and as each breath departs, count silently to four once again. This habit should help to slow you down and it will also help you to develop a steady pace and rhythm to your breathing. When you are ready, begin to read, and then mull over, the story of Nicodemus.

First begin to picture the scene as Nicodemus himself must have experienced it. We are told that this man was a leader of his people and must have regularly heard about this new guru, Jesus, who had come to the area.

While others were threatened and disturbed by this new figure, Nicodemus was enthralled. He knew that he wanted and needed to meet this astounding individual.

Instead of allowing those wishes to stay dormant, Nicodemus made it his business to search out Jesus for himself. So many others were finding hope and life in this new guru, and Nicodemus, too, felt that he should find out what all the excitement was about.

Being a leader, he had prudence. He waited until it was dark before he sought Jesus out. He could see no point in ruining his own reputation if Jesus turned out to be a fraud or imposter.

So go with Nicodemus now as he makes his way to the unfamiliar area of town where he has heard Jesus might be found.

Watch him as he makes his way warily, casting the occasional glance behind to make sure he is not being followed. Note how he pulls his cloak over his face to disguise his identity. Listen as he mutters to himself and questions his own sanity and folly.

Often enough he has to hide both his thoughts and feelings, even to himself. Deep down, he knows that he is not truly happy. There's a sort of restlessness inside. He's searching for something – but what that 'something' is he doesn't know.

In your imagination, keep your eyes locked on Nicodemus as he asks bystanders if they know where Jesus might be staying. Finally, one answers in the affirmative and Nicodemus follows the directions he's given.

Stay with him as he spots Jesus and makes his way over. Watch the surprise on Jesus' face as he sees who has come to visit him. Visits from such dignitaries are rare. Usually the holders of powerful positions are his enemies. But this one seems different. Watch Jesus listening to Nicodemus. Note how he ponders the questions and frames suitable replies in his mind.

You are some little distance away so you can scarcely hear the conversation. At length you can just make out Jesus expressing his thanks to Nicodemus for the risk he has taken. You may also hear him tell Nicodemus that his world isolates him from the experience, sufferings and pain of the poor. He knows it is difficult for Nicodemus to feel their pain and isolation but you can see that a realisation is slowly coming to the night visitor that the path ahead will not be easy. If he can achieve at least part of the challenge that is being put before him, however, perhaps great inner life might result. You hear Jesus' words. 'Nicodemus, would you like to have as much care and concern for those around you as you have for yourself?' Watch his panic as he realises the implications of the question put to him. He is being asked to leave his comfortable existence and step out in a new direction.

Suddenly, Jesus turns his gaze away from Nicodemus and looks towards you. Hear the question coming from Jesus' mouth in your direction. 'And you – would also like to be born again?'

Try to ponder that question for yourself and think about what its answer might demand of you. Will you need to refocus your vision or prejudices? Look at those around you and see what their needs might be. Do you want to be born again? Only one person can answer that question.

St Ignatius of Loyola recommended that we take a look – for a short time each day – at what is going on in our lives. This form of prayer is usually called the Examen, and a number of versions, including this one based on an example by the Linn brothers and friends in the United States, might prove helpful.

Preparation

Light a candle and imagine yourself in a favourite place with someone you love and trust. This might be a friend, or Jesus, or God – as you understand God.

Put your feet flat on the floor; take a few deep breaths from the bottom of your toes, up through your legs, your abdominal muscles and your chest. Breathe in that unconditional love and, when you breathe out, fill the space around you with it.

Place your hand on your heart and ask Jesus to bring your heart back to the moment today for which you are most grateful. If you could relive one moment, what would it be? When were you able to give and receive love and thanks today?

Ask yourself what was said and done in that moment that made it so special. Breathe in the gratitude you felt and receive life again from that moment.

Ask Jesus to bring to your heart the moment today for which you are least grateful. When were you least able to give and receive love? Ask yourself what was said and done in that moment that made it so difficult. Be with whatever you feel without trying to change or fix it in any way. You may wish to take deep breaths and let God's love fill you just as you are.

Give thanks for whatever you have experienced. If possible, share with a friend as much as you can of what has just happened.

Tell your friend what you are most grateful for ... and what you are least grateful for. These are two very important questions.

Put another way – when did you feel most alive today and when did you most feel life draining out of you?

When were you happiest today and when were you saddest?

What was today's high (or low) point?

How can you increase the chances of having a similar high point tomorrow?

Finish with the Lord's Prayer.

Sit comfortably with your eyes closed. Let your awareness move down into the centre of your body and notice what you feel there.

Get in touch with an experience of desolation or consolation.

Ask yourself if you want to listen to this part of yourself right now.

If it is okay to spend some time with this area of your life, take a few moments to create a loving atmosphere where it will feel safe to speak to yourself.

Now let yourself down into how this whole thing feels inside you. Where in your body do you especially experience it? Chest, stomach, throat?

Care for this feeling and see if it wants to tell you about itself. Where did it come from? What does it need?

Whatever comes, reach out to care for it without trying to change it or fix it. Ask Jesus or a trusted friend to come and help you care for it.

Tell this part of you that you will come back at another time and listen to it some more.

Try to see, before finishing, if your body feels differently compared to when you began. Are you carrying this issue differently in your body?

Our emphasis on hearing the story behind our desolation is consistent with the teaching of great spiritual writers like St Ignatius. When, for example, we follow his suggestion to look at the beginning, middle and end of any temptation, or his suggestion to discover the roots of what he called 'sin', we are beginning to listen to the story of our desolation. Any process can help reveal the story of our desolation if it puts us in touch with what started it (the beginning), what keeps it going now (the middle) and what needs to be resolved (the end).

Often what your desolation most wants to say to you is, 'I need you to do more of what consistently brings you the most consolation.' Thus, our consolation may reveal to us (and help meet) the unmet need behind our desolation.

The criterion for hearing the voice of God is the willingness to become aware. For St Ignatius, 'one day his eyes were opened a little and he began to wonder at the difference between consolation and desolation and to reflect on it'.

Anthony de Mello used to say that a person cannot sin in awareness. We understand this to mean that God is always speaking within us, and the more aware we become, the better chance we have of hearing God's voice. The Examen helps us hear the voice of God because, in paying attention to consolation and desolation, we become aware.

What seems life-giving about the practice of the Examen for you and what doesn't?

'What am I doing because I enjoy it and what am I doing because I should?'

Jesus said, 'Seek and you shall find, knock and the door will open to you.'

In this meditation you want to look at a situation or difficulty that has been on your mind recently.

Settle yourself and take time out. Use one of the breathing exercises to help with inner quietness.

Now, in your imagination, picture yourself on a mountainside. You have heard that a spiritual guide resides here.

Imagine yourself sitting down in a particular spot on the mountain and gazing out in front of you. Gradually, this wise and compassionate being materialises in the space in front of you. It might appear as Jesus, or a counsellor, or simply as an older and wiser version of yourself.

Spend a few minutes with this figure ... in silence. If the figure seems critical of you, then he or she not the one you're looking for – so ask the figure to step aside and invite the real counsellor/friend/guide to appear.

Know that this person has your best interests at heart and sense his or her generosity towards you as you receive what is offered. Take time to ask a few questions or discuss any issue that has been bothering you lately. Don't rush along, but pause and receive any answers the guide might wish to present. Give the process time and watch as the guide develops a voice of its own.

Try to feel at home with the guide and ask for help to discover the qualities or answers you feel you need right now.

When you feel the process has gone on as long as you want, thank the guide for spending time with you and ask to meet again in the future.

Come back to this present time and place ...reflect on the experience ...and ponder the answers/insights/gifts you have been given.

5

BUILD ON WHAT YOU'VE GOT

The real voyage of discovery consists not in seeking new land-scapes but in having new eyes.
Marcel Proust

It was Easter Sunday, and I was due to say the mid-morning Mass in my local parish. As you might expect, I had been thinking for some days about what theme might be appropriate for the season. Something about the relationship between Jesus and his Father seemed like a good place to begin, but I felt drawn in another direction. My mother had died just a short time previously and the following story is probably greatly influenced by that fact. My thoughts and feelings were all over the place but were generally centred around the effect mothers have – or can have – on their children.

I'm a chaplain and student adviser in one of Ireland's universities, and as I was preparing that Easter sermon, a parent of one of our students died. I knew immediately that I wanted to attend the funeral even though it was going to take place quite some distance from my home base and I was still very raw around the whole area of death and dying. That very fact gave a real impact to the story I was shortly to hear. I arrived in the student's home village shortly before his mother's service was about to begin and waited for proceedings to start.

It wasn't long before the local priest came out onto the altar. Straight away, he exuded presence. He was a big man, impressive, with a Friar Tuck air about him, and he immediately settled the crowd. He had a lovely way of reaching out to the family in their time of pain and both what he said – and the way he said it – reached out to me also. As he talked, he brought us back to his own time as a trainee priest and filled in the scene for his listeners. One summer, while he was still a seminarian in his final student year, he was sent on placement to this very parish. His placement had a definite purpose – it was to observe, learn and help the local clergy in so far as he could. The parish team consisted of a parish priest and curate but just before his arrival the older priest had been taken ill and was going to be away in hospital for the entire summer. The curate, delighted to receive a helper who might lighten his load, told our young seminarian that the sick priest's car was going to be idle for the next few months and the young visitor might as well make use of it to get out on parish visits. Needless to say, the young seminarian was delighted. Never having been the proud owner of a vehicle himself, he went out to the garage to inspect his mode of transport. To his surprise and delight, he found he was now the proud possessor of a top-class motor car – a Rover Supreme to be exact. As he related the story, the priest – now a parish priest himself – recounted how he whizzed around the highways and byways in his elegant vehicle over the next few days. The parish work was heavy and, patting his rather bulky stomach as he recalled the experience for us, he went on to explain that one of his greatest delights after a particularly hard day was to drive to the local village two or three miles away where – to use his own phrase – the locals rejoiced in one of the greatest 'fish and chippers' in the country.

All went swimmingly until one particularly onerous day. Meetings piled up, schools had to be visited, problems of one sort or another came rushing at him from every direction. As evening approached he decided that now, more than ever, he deserved one of those famous fish suppers, so he hopped into the parish priest's car and set off at a fast clip to the chipper. 'I don't know exactly what happened,' he told us, 'but I misjudged either my speed or the angle of a bend in the road and ended up taking the corner too sharply and also taking a sizeable slice out of the side of the car.' As might be expected, the poor man nearly dropped dead with shock. Being only a student, any hope he had of ever getting a position in that parish or with that parish priest had, in his mind, vanished.

He paused for a moment in his tale and then turned to us, the congregation. 'Do you think my first move after the accident was to phone the parish priest? No, it was not! Or perhaps you think I got on to the police to let them know that an accident had occurred. Wrong again! No, I got on to my mother and related my misfortune to her.' She asked first had I killed or injured anybody. 'No.' Well, perhaps I had hurt myself? When she heard that this was not the case either and that it was the magnificent parish priest's car that had come off worst in the whole incident her response was, 'Thank God, sure it's only an auld car and they can always be replaced.'

'I learned that day where true support and love really lie,' the priest told us, 'for mothers are vital, and if you happen to have been given a particularly outstanding one, it's wise to stop and acknowledge the grace you have been given and give thanks for the fact as well.' As his mother had kept the priest going during his hour of desperation, so the risen Christ keeps us afloat if we ask for his assistance during our times of trial. It's important to remember the gifts we have been given, who gave them, and how we can use the inheritance that has been entrusted to us if faith and prayer are not to slowly dribble away.

It's easy in today's climate to forget or devalue what our faith has given us. An enquiry arrived on my desk recently and it came from an unlikely source. A student branch of the Legion of Mary in our university was having its induction night for newcomers and needed a priest to welcome and bless their new entrants. I was asked to perform the task – and I have to come clean here. I don't know too much about the Legion of Mary, and though I wouldn't admit it in public, I suppose the organisation, in my mind, has a slightly

'Holy Mary' image to it. Years ago, I used to watch some of their more senior members passing out prayer leaflets to all sorts of crazy-looking youths, punk rockers, stoned-looking teenagers and other youngsters each Saturday in Dublin's city centre. As the leaflets were being given out, I didn't know whether to be mortified by the sniggering and abuse they received or spellbound with admiration for the courage that the Legion members displayed as they went about their work. Anyway, let me get back to the induction evening being held for new members in the university. To make it a bit special, the Legion had invited one of their recently retired members to come along and give a talk to the assembled multitude. They had also given her free rein with regard to the subject of her address, and as she had only recently completed her studies she had decided to speak about how she had got on in college. As soon as she walked into the room I noticed that she didn't exactly fit my profile of what a Legion of Mary member would look like. I wondered what had persuaded her to become a Legion member and hoped she might say something about that. She did not disappoint. Right at the start she explained that she was going to focus on this very subject so I began to sit up and take notice.

It's only fair before we begin that I say something about the way the speaker presented herself. She was about twenty-four years of age, was about as snappily turned out as you can imagine, and as soon as she opened her mouth you could tell she was as sharp as a new pin. She didn't exactly fit my profile of what Legion of Mary members might look like, although perhaps that says a good deal more about me than about Legion members. She began by telling us that she had chosen law as her field of study. Since early childhood she had always been fascinated by it. She knew that she needed really high points to gain entry to the course but that did not particularly bother her as she had always come close to the top of her class.

In college, everything went pretty much as expected – and as she had hoped – during her first three years. Top marks came easily. Her reputation for excellence among lecturers and fellow students seemed secure. It was in her fourth year of study that trouble started and brought about a rude awakening. Somehow or other distractions of all sorts came along. Her marks – and her life – began to unravel. Things got so desperate that she honestly believed that not only was she not going to get the first-class honours she expected and hoped for but, if the truth be told, she was unlikely to get any distinctions at all. Failing the course became a distinct possibility.

It was at that point that her mother came into the story, so the patron saint of mothers – whoever that may be – can now stand up and take a bow. In fact all mothers can probably begin to feel good about themselves, for this particular mother obviously had a deep faith but she wasn't going to offer easy solutions to difficult problems. When the daughter explained the pickle she was in and the fact that recent results indicated she was unlikely to pass her final exams, the mother leapt into action. 'I'll pray for your success, and I don't doubt that my prayers will be answered, but I'll do it only if you agree to two things. Firstly, you have to cut out all other distractions and get back to your books straight away, and secondly, I want you to join the Legion of Mary for a year. Those are my terms, and the reason I strike such a hard bargain is that I need to beat a path to Our Lady's door right now because her best efforts are going to be needed from now until exam time if we're to get what we're looking for.' The mother concluded by saying she was so confident that the request would be granted that she would not make her daughter fulfil her part of the bargain if the exam results did not meet her daughter's expectations and a distinction was not achieved.

Our speaker told us that this deal seemed reasonable to her. 'To tell the truth, I had little enough chance of a pass, let alone of gaining a distinction,' she told us, 'so I wasn't too worried about having to pay the price. I committed myself to the arrangement and I don't have to tell you what happened because you can see it standing before you. The results arrived and I found that the excellent result I had dreamed of had in fact materialised. I also remembered the pact I had made and knew I had to stick to it. The very next week I came to the Legion meeting and asked for an application form. That's how I became a member – even if a slightly unwilling one – and that's how I'm here this evening.'

She went on to explain that shortly after all this happened, her Legion presidium in the university invited a priest from an English parish to come and speak to their group. He explained that he hoped to run a week-long retreat in his area and invited any Legion members who were there that evening to be part of the experience. If they were willing to volunteer, he would have them over the next summer to conduct this retreat with his parishioners. Slightly to her own amazement, she volunteered. The decision changed her life – and faith. 'I became a doer, rather than an observer', was the way she put it herself. 'Whilst before I had sat at the feet of others and been passive, now I was actually engaged. I was on the front line – totally committed. Those we visited said what our visits meant to them. I couldn't believe it. We were having a real effect on them, their lives, and their faith, and I think they were telling the truth. I never actually thought that any actions of mine could inspire others in their faith. To a certain extent I can hardly believe it still. But deep down, I know it's true.'

When I began to think about her story afterwards, I started to realise that her mother's belief and request had influenced our speaker powerfully. Perhaps parents or friends don't so much pass on the faith as encourage it within us, for it may be that the trust and courage they display in their own lives inspire us to hook into something of the faith and heritage that is being offered to us by God. Most of us know, at some level or another, that we haven't fulfilled and achieved our full capability. Some – and Anthony de Mello would say most – of our true potential has been left unused and under-developed. Occasionally, we have seen ourselves at our best moments – times when we stand tall and courageous – but this only highlights the fact that neglecting to make use of our inherited gifts has brought forth in us narrowness, insensitivity, meanness and self-destructive tendencies that lead to pain and disappointment for others and ourselves.

If we forget to value our birthright and build on it, it's easy for us to become disillusioned and discouraged. It's worth noting that a public opinion poll taken in 1994 by the National Opinion Research Centre shows that many of us start out in life with high hopes and expectations and that over half of all adults in their twenties find their lives 'exciting'. That sounds promising; but by the time people reach their forties, things have already begun to deteriorate. The proportion of those thinking things are going well at that age has already dipped to forty-six per cent and by the time we have reached the age of sixty, only thirty-five per cent feel as positive as they did. Unless we learn to appreciate what we have been given in faith areas and can find a deeper meaning in life, then things begin to look increasingly grim. Our expectations are likely to diminish and our ability to help and inspire others is likely to founder.

Before beginning this exercise it is often a good idea to find a suitable time in your day when you can be alone, quiet and at peace. Many find early in the day before distractions set in a good time or perhaps you might be happier choosing the late evening when your labours are finished.

Choose a suitable location – quiet and undisturbed. Allocate about twenty minutes for the exercise and hope to increase this time to thirty or forty minutes as you get more used to the process.

Settle yourself in a seated position on a straight-backed chair and place your hands in your lap.

Close your eyes and relax.

Breathe in and out deeply and feel your whole upper body filling with air. Build up a gentle and rhythmic pace of breathing – that should help you to relax. Draw the air in through your nostrils and imagine it coming to the back of your mouth and hitting the back of your throat before coming down through your windpipe and towards your shoulder area. Then allow it to move slowly downwards through your arms and into your fingers. Imagine your chest area filling with air and then notice the air circling around your backbone and travelling down to the pit of your stomach. (If you place your hand over the centre of your stomach you should be able to feel it reaching your belly button.)

As you breathe inwards and outwards, it may help to pace yourself if you count slowly and silently as you breathe in and out. Count slowly to four as you breathe in, and, after a short pause, count a further four beats as you breathe gently out. This should help you to slow down in breathing and produce a heightened, mind-calming effect.

With your eyes closed, see if you can become aware of the sensations that present themselves. Notice the air as you breathe in and out. Recognise the coolness of this substance on each inward breath and the slightly warmer feel as you breathe out through your mouth.

Keep up that quiet, gentle pattern of breathing for a few minutes. When you feel suitably still and quiet, imagine Christ is sitting there beside you and spend a few moments alone with him.

Before you begin this exercise, think about the story Tony de Mello told while giving a retreat in Ireland. He said that he himself often experienced difficulty praying, particularly during his years of formation as a Jesuit. During a retreat he made in his youth, the retreat director had asked him, 'How do you pray?' The question forced him to give some thought to his own prayer practice so he began to explain his method. He said that he first chose a scriptural text and prepared two or three points from the passage. Next, he reminded himself that the Lord is present at these times to offer grace and hope and then he started with the first point that he wanted to pray about in the passage. He was honest enough to admit that it was usually not long after that before he got distracted. The retreat director then asked what he did next. 'Well, I start over again and think about what went wrong.' The retreat director said, 'You're not praying – all you are doing is thinking.' He told him to begin with a Hail Mary and imagine that he was saying something to Our Lady. Well, that seemed simple enough to de Mello so he took his advice and said he never had difficulty with prayer after that. He told us that people usually have difficulty with prayer for one of the following reasons:

They go there to think.
They get distracted.
They don't know what to do with themselves.

Go to your place of prayer.
Imagine Our Lady is there beside you.
Slowly repeat the lines of the Hail Mary, one after the other.

Do it very slowly.
Just dwell on each line and let it soak into your heart.
Be content with whatever emerges during the prayer time.

See how it works for you.

Light a candle and choose a time and place for prayer. Assume a suit-able position and sit down. Then try to get your head, neck and chest in alignment.

Start by focusing on your heart area, somewhere close to the middle of your chest, and then, with your mouth closed, breathe in and out.

Keep your attention on that same central point as if you were using it to breathe in and out, and maintain a pace for your breathing that is slow, deep and regular.

Sometimes it helps to imagine that the room you are praying in is filled with a coloured mist – I find a yellow or golden tinge works best for me, but you can choose whatever colour best suits your mood. As you breathe in and out, try to imagine you are drawing this mist deep within you. In a sense, you are drawing the breath or spirit of God into yourself and asking that it might infuse your being.

So, as you breathe, make a prayer and ask that the grace you are looking for may be given to you during this reflective time. On each outbreath request that anything that may be blocking God's presence (such as tiredness, frustration, guilt, anger or pain) may be held at bay, at least for these few minutes.

Next, form a picture in your mind as you visualise this coloured mist which is entering your being. It often helps if you have your eyes almost closed at this time. Through those almost closed eyes you can see splinters of golden light rising up from the candle. I often think of these as signs of the Holy Spirit making its presence felt. Allow this presence to settle close to your heart where it takes on a life of its own in your imagination and begins to radiate light and peace to those it touches.

Now, slowly, allow this sense of the Holy Spirit within you to grow in size. With time, it will begin to fill you with its presence and, as it does, try to experience a sense of the Spirit coming down upon you with its gifts of hope and encouragement.

When you feel ready, send a blessed feeling out to those who have asked you to pray for them. Send that same blessing out to those who are ill, lonely, afraid or without hope.

Ask the Spirit to bring to those others the serenity he or she is bringing to you.

'It will be as when a man who was going on a journey called in his servants and entrusted his possessions to them. To one he gave five talents, to another, two, to another, one – to each according to his ability. Then he went away. Immediately, the one who received five talents traded with them and made another five. Likewise, the one who received two talents made another two. But the man who received one talent went off and dug a hole in the ground and went off and buried his master's money. After a long time, the master of those servants came back and settled accounts with them. The one who had received five talents came forward, bringing the additional five. He said, "Master, you gave me five talents. See, I have made five more." His master said, "Well done, my good and faithful servant. Since you were faithful in small matters, I will give you great responsibilities. Come and share your master's joy." Then the one who had received two talents also came forward and said, "Master, you gave me two talents. See, I have made two more." His master said to him, "Well done, my good and faithful servant. Since you were faithful in small matters, I will give you great responsibilities. Come, share your master's joy." Then the one who had received the one talent came forward and said, "Master, I knew you were a demanding person, harvesting where you did not plant and gathering where you did not scatter; so out of fear I went off and buried your talent in the ground. Here it is back." His master said to him in reply, "You wicked, lazy servant! So you knew that I harvest where I did not plant, and gather where I did not scatter. Should you not then have put my money in the bank so that I could have got it back with interest on my return? No then, take the talent from him and give it to the one with ten, for to everyone who had, more will be given and he will grow rich. But from the one who has not, even what he has will be taken away. And throw this useless servant into the darkness outside where there will be wailing and grinding of teeth.'"

Begin your meditation by trying to remember that when you are tense, worked-up, keyed-up or knotted-up your body realises it and sends your blood pressure soaring. Your breathing becomes irregular and your whole physical, mental and emotional being suffers. You need to wind down, calm down and settle down in order to relax and get what you can from the gospel story. Ponder what the Lord may be trying to say to you.

Phase One: Reading
Read the gospel story and prepare yourself for prayer. Then begin, thinking about the three characters in the story who were given talents. Look at the different ways in which they used those gifts.

After some time, allow your imagination to place you in the gospel scene as it is described.

What talents do you think you have been given by God?

How have you used them?

Were you generous or mean in their use?

Some people don't recognise their own talents. Do you recognise yours?

The character who was cursed in the story was not the one who had tried and failed but the one who had been too fearful to risk using his talents in the first place. Try saying to yourself, 'I'd rather have tried and failed than not to have tried at all.'

Some people have a great gift for developing the gifts of others. Have I drawn out the talents of those around me during the past months?

If I have, I give thanks for that fact. If I have not, I ask that I may be a greater giver of encouragement in the future.

When reading this gospel, I don't really read it like a book but rather a letter that God might send me. I read it slowly, pausing when necessary and allowing time for the thought or message to sink in. I read quietly, trying to make the experience intimate and prayerful. As I finish the reading, I pick out a thought or feeling that may have struck me as I read. This becomes the bridge to the second phase of my prayer experience – the listening phase.

Phase Two: Listening

Hearing something read out loud by someone else heightens your appreciation of the passage and may assist you in understanding and remembering the ideas presented. This method is modelled by Our Lady when she ponders deeply the words that the angel Gabriel had spoken to her. During the listening phase, we reflect= upon what we have just read. We have had the experience, and now we're looking for the meaning.

Phase Three: Speaking

Here you might be helped by imagining Jesus as a companion walking by your side or sitting close by. Try to think of how two close friends might feel at ease when they are close to one another – and model the relationship between yourself and Jesus in that manner.

EXERCISE FIVE: REVIEW YOUR PRAYER

- Did the prayer time go well or badly?
- Was I too tired?
- Was the place too noisy?
- Can I avoid these difficulties next time?
- Did I manage to enter into a prayerful disposition?
- Did I compose myself well beforehand?
- Can I use any insights gained on future occasions?
- Did I prepare carefully?
- Did I rush the session?
- Might I spend a little more time opening myself up to God at the beginning?
- What was the subject matter of my prayer?
- How much of the scripture passage did I get through?
- Do I need to go back over any section?
- What insights did I have?
- Was there anything in my prayer that disturbed me?
- Did I understand why I was troubled at that particular point?
- Was there any point at which I seemed to come up against a block?
- Is there something here that needs looking at and working on within myself?
- Did I manage to address myself directly to God – with words or without words?
- When I stopped was there more that could have been fruitfully explored?
- When do I plan to make my next prayer period?
- What would I like to use as material for that?
- Would it be good to continue with the theme I have been working on?

6

CLEVER AS A FOX

A man is happy so long as he chooses to be happy.
Alexander Solzhenitsyn

Anthony de Mello usually looked like he was enjoying life. Therefore, he might well have been encouraged by a friend of mine who recently cheered me up with a good story. She had decided that after finishing school she was going to join a religious order. Shortly before she did so, an old uncle of hers who was a missionary priest visited her home. When she told him of her plans and how she was looking with excitement towards religious life, he was delighted, but felt he had to give a little advice. He mentioned that in his view people he met could be divided into two categories. He had observed over many seasons the guests who came regularly to the retreat centre in Rome where he was based. Such visitors, he explained, had one of two views about the city. They either felt that the capital was magical, or they thought it was a disgrace. The 'magical' brigade was completely captivated by the magnificence of the metropolis as they cast their gaze towards the skies. The very beauty that surrounded them took their breath away. On the other hand, those who felt the place was a disgrace had looked at their surroundings in an entirely different manner. Their eyes looked downwards and they were disgusted by the squalor and filth they found around their feet. They thought Rome was just about the dirtiest city they had ever encountered. When her uncle, the Franciscan, gave my friend his best wisdom, he advised that she should 'Look upwards and try to keep your gaze fixed on the goodness and beauty you encounter in life – for if you allow your vision to be dragged downwards, you will only be discouraged by the squalor of the gutter and by the worst excesses that mankind is capable of.'

Her story was reinforced a few days later as I prepared for a Mass I was due to offer at the university where I work as a chaplain. For months, wave after wave of horrific news about the Church and its decision-makers had been pouring forth. Clearly I was going to have to say something about these events and I wasn't looking forward to it. Bad news, scandals, horror stories and worse have been coming at us thick and fast in recent times and as a priest I find myself having to speak on the Church's behalf. It's not a task anyone is likely to relish – certainly I don't – and it's often hard enough to understand why Church decisions were taken in the way they were and even harder to explain or defend the rationale behind those decisions to others. We assembled, and the audience for the Mass was mainly university students. When sermon time came, I began to focus on the question that has been much in my mind of late. What effect has this constant drip-drip of defamatory outpourings been having on the faith lives of our students? Have they themselves been able to look at this – and with what result? I knew these questions would be difficult for them and, in return, I promised to share what effect these last months have had on me – in so far as I could work that out. The experience was revealing. As the students talked, one after another said that they felt reasonably secure in their faith. They valued what they had been given in their youth and were going to stick with their beliefs. They nearly all added that they hoped to have children in the future and intended to bring them up as Catholics – but were unsure whether this would in fact happen. Younger people today, they feared – without the secure faith foundations they themselves had been given – may well abandon membership of any type of institutional church. When my turn came to speak, I talked about having to get up, time after time, before congregation after congregation and attempt to speak. In so far as I knew what I felt and could articulate it, my reactions to the seedy revelations about what had been going on within our Church induced in me feelings of shame and embarrassment. To this mix I added words of apology and remorse towards those who had suffered and expressed a good measure of rage towards those who had sullied the good name of the Church. As I did so, I called to mind excellent ambassadors of Christ – many of them teachers I had at school – that I had known myself. A lot of these are now dead, but I feel certain that they would be turning in their graves if they knew how the memory of them had been sullied and dragged through the dirt by recent revelations. I suspected many of those listening were probably feeling confused and dejected. As I had been encouraged by the story of the old Franciscan and his advice to keep one's gaze fixed on what inspires and not let oneself become depressed by the less than edifying scandals that might also come to one's notice, I had determined to share the uncle's story with the congregation in the hope that it might help some who found themselves in a dark place.

When we came to the end of the service, one woman came up to me. She had clearly taken in everything and wanted to share her own insights with me. Her first comment was gently delivered but she pointed out that she was afraid I was looking in the wrong direction or the wrong place for answers. She suggested that if one worries about the Church as an institution, and places too much hope in the individuals that make up that Church and how well they act, one leaves oneself open to major disappointment. Much wiser, she suggested, to keep your eyes on Christ and his goodness and see where that leads you. Her second contribution was even more helpful to me because she knew I liked stories – particularly ones that are true – and she was happy to share hers with me. She explained that she came from a rural background and her family kept peacocks on their land. She recounted how these birds were terrified by a local fox and high-tailed it into the nearest trees whenever the fox made its nightly rounds of their farmstead. The peacocks were given some warning of the visits, however, because the fox usually barked as it approached each evening and stayed away if, as was always the case, it heard an answering challenge to its inquiry from the farm's very reliable guard dog. However, this idyllic state of affairs was destined to change.

Some little time previously the dog fell sick and was brought to the vet for a check-up. As there was some question as to what exactly was the matter with him, the vet decided to hold the dog for a few days to try to get to the root of the problem. Then, and only then, did the fox seize his opportunity. The very next evening, as the clever creature made his nightly rounds and came close to the family farm, he sounded his usual call. For once, no warning growl warned him off and so he made his way boldly forward. He came right into the inner yard itself and found the peacocks had taken up their positions where he expected they might be. His arrival caused a considerable commotion among the birds. Despite the fact that they were not the smartest creatures alive, the peacocks had got an inkling of his approach and had managed individually to scramble up six trees that were dotted around the yard. Thus the fox found to his disappointment that each peacock was now safely perched in its own tree. For some time, the fox sat below, looking up longingly at the tantalising treats above, but he could think of no way to get up at them. He wasn't an animal who gave up easily, however.

The very next night he returned. Again his unanswered bark told him that no guard dog was at home. This time when he came into the yard he again found each peacock perched in its own tree but now he changed his tactic. He targeted one tree and sat beneath it. When he had the full attention of the individual above, he made his move. As the peacock glanced down at the perils below, the fox fixed it with a stare. When he was certain that he had created a terrified eye-to-eye contact, the fox slowly began to circle around the base of the tree. The foolish bird above, fixated on this danger below, swivelled its head around and around to keep the fox in view. After a few minutes it became disoriented, fell out of the tree and was quickly consumed. On subsequent nights, the five other peacocks were fooled by exactly the same trick. They also perished. They had allowed themselves to become fixated by the catastrophe below them rather than looking at the splendour and safety above. They might have done better if they had followed the advice offered by the old Franciscan.

I've mentioned that it's often not easy to stay positive when we see some of the turmoil around us, particularly in Church affairs. Before he left his disciples Christ said to them that it was important that he departed because otherwise they might never grow up, nor gain the ability to confront what they needed to face in life. Otherwise the disciples might not learn how to look up to the Spirit for inspiration rather than be dragged down in desolation by the goings-on taking place around them. Perhaps Christ doesn't always answer our prayer straight away or in the way we might wish because he needs us to mature. He wants us to strike out on our own and to grow up. That's what we are made for.

They say that boats are safest when they are in harbour. Perhaps they are, but that's not what sailing vessels were created for. They will never achieve anything if they do not set sail. That's also true for us and was equally true for the apostles, but to see in which direction we need to move and what new areas of life might produce growth for us is not too easy – and requires time. The Irish writer and poet Brendan Kennelly, commenting on new trends in modern society, said nobody seems to have time nowadays to see what is really going on. Neither do they have the leisure to look seriously at themselves. In present-day Ireland he sees disturbing trends which have serious implications for us all. Haste, hurry, hassle and stress seem to be the new kids on the block – the new gods in our lives, if you like. Instead of looking at our values and beliefs in a long and leisurely fashion, we tend to give them brief, snappy glances. These quick glimpses give us insufficient time to gauge what is worth while before we hasten on – half blind – with our furious activity. Kennelly pointed out that we live in a world of glimpses, and he determined that for himself at least he would write poems based on this fact. He suggested that for him a glimpse is a passing, flashing and momentary view of a situation and is necessarily incomplete. He said he would begin to take time off to meditate on the brief glimpses he could remember of a relatively distant past life. 'As I got used to glimpsing, I found myself paying more accurate attention to what is really going on. I began to see that our lives are full of glimpsed pictures of all kinds. I believe that good poems are flashes of light in the darkness of the heart and mind.'

Trying to gain light in the darkness of our hearts and minds is important and it only happens when we create space for reflection. Many resonate with the artist J. M. W. Turner when he told a story about the time he tried to sell a picture of his entitled Fingal's Cave. The potential buyer mentioned that the landscape in question seemed to him to be rather indistinct – fuzzy, you might say. 'Indistinctness is my forte,' was Turner's response, and it might also be ours when we come to think about present-day values. To clarify these standards for ourselves, we may need to avail of a suggestion made by both Pascal and Pythagoras. These two astute observers of humankind provide a valuable lesson about a practice that is not popularly encouraged in our culture today. They hint that there is tremendous value in creating inner space each day by carving out times of silence and introspection. You may well be struck by the need for this if you treat yourself to a train journey. As soon as you take your seat, just glance around. Your carriage may be filled, the countryside may be enchanting, but a large percentage of your fellow travellers are likely to have their attention anywhere but in the here and now. They will probably be absorbed with their mobile phones, texting their friends, interacting on social media, playing games or listening to music, all activities that pull them away from what is taking place in their immediate vicinity. As James Joyce would have said, they are 'living a long way from their bodies'. The snag is that if we do not find or create time to sift through what is going on around us and work out what might be valuable, patterns of an unhelpful nature may build up rapidly. Without reflective time, we may never be able to process what is going on within – or do anything about it. Such space and time seems like a luxury but Anthony de Mello never felt that it was. He believed that if we postpone finding time for reflection, we do so at our peril.

I recall John O'Donohue, the Irish philosopher, making similar observations about the lack of reflective time he noticed in his life and in the lives of others right from his student days. He remembered the first evening he arrived in Tübingen, where he did his post-graduate work. It was a German town, but despite his excitement he had the presence of mind to say to himself, 'Look at this place very carefully. You'll never see it again in the same way as you're seeing it now in your first raw unprogrammed encounter with it.' He knew that he needed to step back from the situation he found himself in and view the experience from a distance if he was to get things into perspective. Sometimes this can only be done by taking time out at regular intervals and looking back over how things have been going for us. In baseball matches they have a rule that allows time out from the game. It provides a breathing space in which the coach and players can look back at the action and study what patterns have appeared. In the hurly-burly of regular play this is very difficult to do, but taking time out and looking back on what has been going on may achieve it. Let's try a meditation or two that might help the process.

Do I have a system to give thanks for the blessings that God bestows on me daily?

Try this one.

Find a comfortable position.

Hold your spine erect so that your breathing can proceed in a steady fashion.

Take note of the depth and pace of your breathing.

Where does the air flow in to your body?

What is the length of each inhale and exhale and of the pauses between the two?

As you breathe in, allow the air to come right down to the pit of your stomach.

Try to unite your mind with your breath.

Now allow your mind to travel back over the last twenty-four hours. Ask yourself:

How well do I keep my focus on the good in life, rather than the bad?

What system might I devise to do this better?

Can I recall a time in my life when a cross in my life turned out to be a blessing – or a blessing in disguise?

When was the last time I complimented a colleague or associate? What keeps me from doing this more often?

What is one thing that God has given me, or not given me, that I have taken for granted and for which I should give thanks?

For what three things in my life am I most grateful?

Why these?

Do I feel that God is calling me to take time out at this point?
Or is he asking me to go on at the same pace? Or take a few weeks off?

After reflection, let me decide what God is calling me to do.

EXERCISE TWO: THOUGHT FOR THE DAY

One of our theology professors was famous for saying nothing – or to be more precise, saying very little. He suggested that when we pray with scripture (or it interacts with us), we should take an unusual model as our guide. We should try to act a little like a cow in a field. By that he meant that we should choose a small portion of scriptural text with perhaps just one idea contained within it. Having read the passage, we should chew upon the material we had just found and we should do that for a good long time.

His advice was: keep chewing, until you have extracted all the goodness you can from the section under consideration. You're trying to get every last scrap you can from the text (even though the passage in question may contain a good deal more nourishment than you can absorb.

So, this morning, take a passage of scripture and work with whatever thought arises from it. Don't read many pages. Just take one thought and sit with it for ten or fifteen minutes. The phrase you settle on might be something like, 'Jesus, remember me, when you come into your kingdom.' Allow that thought to stay with you and deepen throughout the day.

St Ignatius expected that God would speak to us through our deepest feelings and yearnings. He believed that 'consolation' or 'desolation' was likely to make itself known. Try this exercise to see if it brings up any feelings for you.

Many experts suggest that beginners should first focus attention on their breathing pattern. The essential action of this practice is very simple. We give continuous attention to the flow of the breath coming in and going out of the body, and whenever we notice our attention straying we gently bring it back to the breath. As we continue doing this we will find our attention becoming deeper and more constant as the mental wandering tends to lessen. As our body relaxes and becomes still, so our mind becomes correspondingly collected, composed and inwardly content.

Sit in a chair with your feet together on the floor in front of you and keep your back straight. Use, as a general principle, the fact that outbreath relaxes while inbreath invigorates.

Breathe in and out deeply and feel your whole upper body filling with air. I often imagine that the room I am working in is filled with a coloured mist – I find a yellow or golden tinge works best for me, but you can choose a colour that you find serene. Draw the air in through the nostrils and imagine it entering your throat, then coming down through your neck and into your shoulder area, then down through your arms until it finds it way down to your fingers. Imagine your chest area filling with the coloured mist and feel how that mist then makes its way, circling down through your body, around your backbone, and from there down to the pit of your stomach. (If you place your hand over your belly button you should be able to feel it travelling down to the core of your being.)

Now put a finger on your pulse and count the beats. Become aware of the rate. Check your pulse frequency and breathe in slowly. After a short pause, breathe gently out, slowly.

I usually find a slow inward count to four on the inbreaths and the outbreaths helps to establish a steady rhythm.

As you practise, you may note that your breathing has slowed down – this often produces a heightened mind-calming effect.

To slow yourself down, count inwardly as you inhale.
As you exhale just count silently – one, two, three, four.
Repeat this exercise several times.

EXERCISE FOUR: LOOKING BACK ON A LIFE

In this prayer session, imagine that you are a seventy-five-year-old coming to the end of your life.

See the events of that past life flash before you. Ask yourself what you are most grateful for.

Are there things that you wish you had done differently?

Pay special attention to the years between your present age and your eventual death.

(One friend of mine who completed this exercise in a prayerful manner said that after the prayer time he knew that he did not want to die in front of a computer screen, so he was going to alter his ways from that day onwards. He wanted to work with people giving workshops or retreats and that was the direction in which he was going to channel his energies in the days ahead.)

Try to discover what you are most grateful for, what you are least grateful for, and what you wish you had done differently in life.

EXERCISE FIVE: THE PRODIGAL SON (LK 15:11–32)

After settling yourself into a prayerful position by means of one of the preparatory exercises, I invite you to recall the famous story of the Prodigal Son from St Luke's Gospel.

'There was a man who had two sons; and the younger of them said to his father, "Father, give me the share of property that falls to me." And he divided his living between them. Not many days later the younger son gathered all he had and took his journey into a far country, and there he squandered his property in loose living. And when he had spent everything, a great famine arose in that country, and he began to be in want. So he went and joined himself to one of the citizens of that country, who sent him into his fields to feed swine. And he would gladly have fed on the pods that the swine ate; and no one gave him anything. But when he came to himself he said, "How many of my father's hired servants have bread enough and to spare but I perish here with hunger! I will arise and go to my father and I will say to him, 'Father, I have sinned against heaven and before you; I am no longer worthy to be called your son; treat me as one of your hired servants.'" And he arose and came to his father. But while he was yet at a distance, his father saw him and had compassion, and ran and embraced him and kissed him. And the son said to him, "Father, I have sinned before heaven and against you; I am no longer worthy to be called your son." But the father said to his servants, "Bring quickly the best robe, and put it on him; and put a ring on his hand and shoes on his feet; and bring the fatted calf and kill it, and let us eat and make merry; for this my son was dead, and is alive again; he was lost, and is found." And they began to make merry.

Now his elder son was in the fields and as he came and drew near to the house, he heard music and dancing. And he called one of the servants and asked him what this meant. And the servant said to him, "Your brother has come, and your father has killed the fatted calf, because he has received him safe and sound." But he was angry and refused to go in. His father came out and entreated him, but he answered his father, "Lo, these many years I have served you, and I never disobeyed your command; yet you never gave me a kid that I might make merry with my friends. But when this son of yours came, who has devoured your living with harlots, you killed for him the fatted calf!" And he said to him, "Son, you are always with me, and all that is mine is yours. It was fitting to make merry and be glad, for your brother was dead and is alive; he was lost, and is found.'"

Place yourself at the scene and go to the father's farmhouse on the night of his son's return. Picture the celebration. Look in through the window at the party going on inside. See the son and the father as they dance around the floor clapping their hands in celebration. Note their joy and remain with them as the night draws to a close.

When all have retired, go to the Prodigal's room and knock at the door. He won't be asleep. His eyes will be shining.

Ask him to tell you his story. Why did he leave home?

What were his adventures along the way and why did he decide to come home?

What helped him come to that decision?

How did he feel when he saw his father running down the road to meet him?

What were his thoughts when he heard the orders being given to bring out the best robe and ring?

And what of the elder brother? How were the two getting along now?

The Prodigal will want to tell you what a wonderful change took place in his heart. As he tells the story, remember it is his father – but also our Father – that he is describing.

If his father could show such love and interest to the prodigal, perhaps your Father is also showing something similar to you?

Try to think about the younger son, born into privilege and wealth. Despite all that, a loving home and high material standards seemed not to be enough. Why did he want to leave?

How much courage did it take to make his request?

What effect did his departure have on his father and his older brother?

Have you ever been tempted to jump the tracks yourself?

Have you let slip your appreciation of the gifts you have been given?

If so, what effect did your decision and your selfishness have on those around you?

EXERCISE SIX: THE PRODIGAL SON (LK 15:11–32)
(ALTERNATIVE VERSION)

Situate the gospel story for yourself, picturing the Prodigal Son with his father.

Now read the gospel story in a slightly different way.

Place yourself alongside the Prodigal Son, and as you look at what's happening in his life, stop off at each stage and see whether the story might be applicable to you.

The Prodigal does not accept himself for some reason.

He dislikes certain of his innate characteristics.

What does he dislike about himself?

Are there elements of your make-up that you are less than happy about?

What are they?

Perhaps they have encouraged feelings of poor self-worth?

Maybe these messages have been dumped upon you by others?

For some months now, the younger son has been uneasy, feeling left out, unsure of what to do, doubtful about his future prospects and quite uncertain about which direction his future life should take. He knows that the longer he feels excluded from his family the more painful life becomes. Perhaps he will never regain feelings of 'all-right-ness' about himself.

The younger son has the courage to take action. He doesn't just slink away during the night. It must take a lot of bravery to face his father.

Have you ever seen the need to take decisive action in your own life which will not go down well with others? Did you take that action? What happened?

For the younger son, things did not turn out for the best. Everything went sour, mostly because of decisions he himself made. In his distress, he had the guts to look at what was going on around him. He was also prepared to eat humble pie after he assessed his situation. He would go back, admit his mistakes, and ask for forgiveness.

Do you take time regularly to assess what is going on in your life? What have you noticed?

Are you happy or are there areas in which things don't seem to be going too well?

The younger son acted when he saw the mess he was in. Do you? If you do not, what is holding you back?

Ask the younger son for some of his fortitude in getting down to the tasks you know need to be done.

The Prodigal will want to tell you what a wonderful change took place in his heart as soon as he decided to return. As he tells the story, remember it is his father – but also your Father – that he is describing.

If his father could show such love and interest to the Prodigal, perhaps your Father is also showing something similar to you?

7

RING THE BELL FOR GRANNY

If the only prayer you ever say in your entire life is 'thank you',
that will be enough.
Meister Eckhart

In the last chapter, we had a look at how those who went before us may have shaped the way we live and pray. Their very lives were a sort of message, but do I know what the message is? One young man seemed to understand without too much difficulty, as I recently found out when I received a phone call out of the blue. It was from a distinguished Irish family and they rang to say that their mother had just passed away. Their local priest happened to be on holiday and they were stuck. Now they were on the phone wondering whether I would be able to step into the breach. Could I conduct their mum's funeral service at short notice?

Even though I had not known their mother, they did not think that would be a problem and they offered to fill me in on details of her life. They suggested that I should visit their house before the funeral itself and say some prayers for the deceased. That would provide an opportunity to fill me in on the facts of her life and give me a few ideas that could be used in her eulogy.

When I arrived at their home, I found family members who were a delight to deal with. As they knew I hadn't known their mother personally, memories of her, and stories about her, came flooding forth. It was clear from the outset that the lady herself had been quite a character and members of the clan certainly painted a vivid picture. It was obvious that she had had great energy and enthusiasm, but mixed these traits with authority and competence. Soon a definite image began to emerge. I was told that she was pretty well known in equestrian circles and was involved in horse shows and gymkhanas up and down the country. It was said of her that her shows ran like clockwork. She put up with no nonsense. Neither horse nor rider was safe if they got out of line.

Their mother possessed a large, old-fashioned school bell which was never too far from her side. She took it to equestrian events and put it to good use. Part of her role was to direct activities in the show ring and make certain that timetables were adhered to. If any horse refused a fence, or acted up, or took longer than allowed to get around the circuit, the result was inevitable. As sure as eggs are eggs, their mother's bell would ring out and the horse in question would be stopped in its tracks. No matter what pleas or tears came from its rider, the said horse's elimination would be announced.

The bell didn't just come into its own at horse shows, however. I learned that it also made regular appearances at home. There, too, it had a useful function. I should mention that the family dwelling was surrounded by large tracts of land. This was great if you were a child as it served as a sort of giant playground. It was not so great, however, if you were a mother trying to gather your children together at meal times. As one of her children explained it, you could, as a child, find yourself rather far from the house at mealtimes, but no matter how far away you were, when the bell was rung by their mother you needed to look lively. If you didn't make it back before the dinner was on the table you were in big trouble.

These stories were related to me in great good humour as we stood around the coffin in the family home before setting out for the church service. One of those standing around was a grandchild, a very bright lad of about ten. It was decided that at the Offertory procession – when gifts to represent her were being brought up to the altar – Mammy's bell would be an ideal item for inclusion. Everyone agreed that her grandchild was a special favourite of hers and that she would have been very pleased to see him being entrusted with the task of bringing up the famous article.

I have to tell you that sometimes at church services unexpected developments take place. Such was the case now. Just before we went out on to the altar, I received word that a distinguished gentleman from the equestrian world had arrived unexpectedly and would like to offer a short eulogy after the communion. Everything was going well and we were nearing the end of the service when I called upon this gentleman to say his few words. He took his place at the podium. A hush came over the crowd. He chose his words carefully, adopted a serious tone, and began to build up a head of steam. The service looked like it would go on a great deal longer than anticipated. It was clearly all a bit much for the grandchild. I don't think he appreciated the new sombre tone or that one sometimes has to adapt to new situations. Right in the middle of the guest speaker's tribute, the lad brought his granny's bell into play and gave it a good solid shake. The effect was electric. For a moment, the grieving congregation took a deep breath and then, almost as one, they exploded. Laughter began to break out on all sides and the solemn tone that had overtaken the proceedings was banished. The distinguished speaker may have been somewhat taken aback to find that his fine sentiments were being so rapidly brought to a conclusion but he knew when he was beaten and had the good sense to bring his efforts to an abrupt end.

When I asked the grandson afterwards what had prompted him to ring the bell he said his grandmother had a few basic principles she laid down for all family members – even the youngest ones. She believed that being born into a special clan gave one advantages – and responsibilities. Privileges came at a price and meant you had to look after those around you. Her ringing of the bell, both at meal times and in the horse show ring, meant that contestants had been given their chance and, 'if you hadn't racked up points in your favour by that point … well, your opportunity was gone.' As the young lad put it, 'I think Granny would have understood only too well that her own time had now come to an end. If she was here herself, she probably would have rung the bell too.

Like the horses in the ring she had gained maximum points in the time allotted to her and I think the Lord is probably pinning a big rosette on her sweater even as we speak.'

It seemed to me at the time – and still does – that this lad had a clear image of his grandmother and knew what her values were. He valued his inheritance and was taking one, at least, of Granny's values on board and using it to enhance his own faith formation. The first thing her life had taught him was that each of us has a limited time here on earth and that we had better use it to the best of our abilities if we want to get to where we are aiming. In becoming mindful of our own inheritance it's no harm to remember that obstacles will emerge to dampen our enthusiasm, for we're not surrounded by Granny's goodness all the time.

Funerals often provide an opportunity for younger members of a family to express their appreciation for more illustrious members of the clan and for what they have given to them. Recently, I was asked to conduct a funeral service in the United States. The deceased lady had all her kinsfolk around her for the farewell liturgy. She was an elderly grandmother and the key people who had cherished her were all present at the event. One of them, Angela, a fourteen-year-old grand-daughter, stands out in my mind for, although nervous, she volunteered this story.

When Angela was about eight, she had been brought up to Colorado on a summer visit by her parents. Her grandmother lived there, in a hillside house overlooking a lake. Clearly, Granny felt that her surroundings were unique and wanted to get this fact across to her granddaughter, but her enthusiasm for the area's natural beauty was not being reciprocated. Much of the grandeur passed over the young girl's head and the quietness of the place bored her. At length, Granny said she had a last and final surprise before Angela went home.

Very late that night, when the whole house was asleep, Angela felt a light touch on her shoulder which woke her. Granny was standing beside her bed. She was told to close her eyes and follow Granny outside where a special present was waiting. The two made their way out to the veranda and Angela was told to lie down – still with her eyes closed. Granny had provided a blanket and, after a few seconds, a moment of magic occurred. Angela was told that she could open her eyes ever so slowly and take a peep. Anticipation was killing her. She did not know what to expect but she trusted Granny and knew that whatever waited would be good. The sight that greeted her was, she said, both magnificent and stunning and one she will remember to her dying day. There, above her, was the most beautiful night sky she ever expects to see. It contained a multitude of dazzling stars, thrown out in a glorious sweep, and topped by a shimmering silver orb – the moon in all its glory. Not only that, but as she turned her head from her prone position on the house's terrace, she saw an exact replica of the night sky mirrored in the lake situated far below.

'I may live a hundred years but I'm unlikely to be given such a special present ever again as Granny gave me that night,' Angela told the congregation. I can testify that her eyes sparkled as she brought the vista to mind. 'From now on,' she said, 'whenever I look at a star in the night sky I'll remember my granny. I will relive that moment and it will be a good reminder to me to squeeze in a prayer of thanks for the beautiful gift she gave me.' Granny had opened up a treasure trove and her granddaughter was determined that it would not be wasted.

We leave messages for all around us whether we like it or not. This came home to me afresh as I watched one of our foremost sports stars, John Giles, being interviewed on Irish television. He's quite elderly now, but the journalist conducting the discussion had clearly not lost his admiration and did a good job of portraying how skilful the ageing star had been. He heaped many gushing statements, one after the other, onto the footballer's head, which meant that poor Giles – who is basically modest by nature – appeared more uncomfortable as each moment went by. Finally, the interviewer suggested that John Giles was probably the most skilful and talented footballer that Ireland has ever produced. He may well have been surprised by the reply because the sportsman said that he wasn't that brilliant at all but he did have one secret. He had been part of a very luminous team with all sorts of virtuoso individuals around him. In truth, they were much more talented than he himself was. However, one thing he had noticed during his career was that during matches, and even during training, they often didn't use the very talent each had been given. He monitored everything and, time after time, noted that what they did not do was use the skills they were individually gifted with. Instead, they seemed to delight in attempting the one thing they could not do. Whereas he knew what he was pretty good at, and utilised that facet of his game time after time, generally staying away from areas of play that he knew from hard experience he could never master, his more naturally gifted colleagues did the exact opposite. They spurned the talents they were lucky enough to have been given – not making full use of the gifts they had – and instead got involved in all sorts of tricks and plays outside their skill range. As a consequence, they often failed to get everything they could from their talents.

EXERCISE ONE: BEST ME AND WORST ME

First, quieten yourself and begin to use your imagination to build up a picture or scene in your head.

Imagine that you are in a theatre.

The place may be a hall you know or one that exists only in your imagination.

It is empty except for yourself. Sit in a middle row seat.

The stage has its curtains drawn back and is empty.

As you sit you suddenly become aware of some movement on stage. Out of the wing on the left-hand side a figure begins to emerge. This is you at your most difficult – your obstructive self.

Picture in your mind's eye your obstructive self as a person.

If you can, imagine having a conversation with your obstructive self. You probably know this self well. It is the one who will not get up in the morning, or who is intimidated by unfamiliar situations, or who is shy or gets rattled easily.

Find out why it acts the way it does.

With compassion, question this self and it will help you out.

(It is only with continuous compassion on your part that this self will reveal its drives and assist you to come to a place where you might dare to look at these behaviours ... the purpose they serve ... and the need for them.) Take time with this.

When you feel both you and your obstructive self have conversed as much as possible, watch as this self slowly begins to fade backwards into the left-hand wing.

Now watch as your positive self begins to emerge from the opposite wing. Note the qualities and personality of this new being.

This is you at your best, at your most energetic, cheerful, kind and constructive.

Ask this person what it needs from you to do its job effectively.

When you are ready, allow your obstructive self to re-emerge and join your best self on stage. Ask them to talk so that, together, they might combine to assist your best self to do its job as effectively as possible.

Remember to ask Jesus to be with you in this scene as you breathe in, and on your outbreaths release whatever seems to be blocking your peace and serenity.

When you feel ready, bring the session to a close.

After preparing yourself, invite all the parts of you, forgotten, loved, hurried, ignored and disliked to gather together in one place. All are welcome. Any busy thoughts or distractions are put to the back of your mind. Now, in your imagination, begin to draw a round table and surround it with chairs.

If you are willing and happy to do so, invite the part of yourself that you call responsible to come and sit at this table. Ask it to say how it is feeling and to unburden any baggage it may be carrying. Let it tell you what role it may be playing in your life.

Next, you may like to ask the best part of you if they would like to come and take a seat at the table. Be open to whoever arrives. Tell them all the things you love about them. If they are not the aspect you are most familiar with, ask them why.

Now, when you are ready, ask the part of yourself that judges others to come to the table. Watch as this part of you enters. Is it stiff and starchy, arrogant or open? Ask what is its role in your life and if it often felt judged. Be open to whatever it may have to say.

Now, invite the part of you that is still a child to come to the table. What age is the child who appears? Does more than one child want to come to your table? Treat this child part of you gently. Give it time to warm to you and to trust you, and ask what it needs in order to feel nurtured. This child part may not be able to respond clearly and you may have to guess what its particular needs are, but ask anyway. Reassure this part of you that at this time you will take care of it.

Now, invite the workaholic part of yourself to take a breather and come to the table. You may or may not be familiar with it. Ask it what it needs to help it to know when to push and when to let go.

If there is a laid-back and lazy part of you, invite it also to make its appearance. It may be reluctant to come forward at all. What does this self have to say? What gift is it willing to give you? What does it need?

Now ask the part of you that is critical of you and the other selves to come along. What does it look like? What or whom does it resemble? Ask it what it needs to be nurtured, what it needs to feel loved and what it fears if it ceases to criticise.

Call upon the most loathed part of yourself – the aspect of yourself that you despise. It's the most secret and most hidden part of your character but well worth reaching if you can. It's the part others don't see and, if they could, you feel, they would not like to be near you at all. Pause for a moment and try to appreciate this part of you.

If you are attempting this prayer exercise in a group, the following questions at the end of your prayer time may be helpful.

What gift can it give you?
Why is it part of you?
What does it need?

Allow your various selves to share.
If you feel able, share your findings with the group.

EXERCISE THREE: A MEDITATION WITH LAZARUS
– UNBIND HIM, AND LET HIM GO. (JN 11:1–44)

Settle yourself in a quiet place and call to mind the phrase of the Buddhist monk and teacher Thich Nhat Hanh:

'Breathing in, I am at peace: breathing out, I let go.'

First, read the gospel account of Jesus and the raising of Lazarus.

Take time to let the passage soak into your being.

When you have done this, the following questions might come to the surface.

How can I love myself more?

How can I forgive myself for past deeds?

What do I need to do next in the area of spiritual growth?

Is this the right place for me to live or work at this moment of my life?

Is this the right relationship for me?

How can I make peace with my body?

How can I create more health and light in my life?

Why don't I get on with my life?

What is my relationship with God right now?

What is appropriate for me in the next few years of my life?

How can I let go of this relationship that has ended?

How can I be comfortable alone?

How can I change the direction I am going in?

What I most yearn for in my retreat time now is … ?

What I fear happening on a retreat is … ?

What I hope will happen on a retreat is … ?

On this retreat I intend to ask myself … ?

What has heart and meaning for me right now ... ?

In the silence, allow these questions to settle within you and see what wisdom or suggestions might come bubbling to the surface.

The story of Martha and Mary in the gospels can be revisited time and again. You will usually find something different to dwell upon each time.

'As Jesus and his disciples were on their way, he entered a village and a woman called Martha welcomed him to her house. She had a sister named Mary who sat down at the Lord's feet to listen to his words. Martha, meanwhile, was busy with all the serving and finally she said, "Lord, don't you care that my sister has left me to do all the serving?" But the Lord answered, "Martha, Martha, you worry and are troubled about many things, whereas only one thing is needed. Mary has chosen the better part and it will not be taken from her."'

Read the story of Martha and Mary and just try to get into the scene. Note how Martha is at home in her house working flat out. So much to do, so little time. That feels a little bit like you are yourself, really. Jesus comes at inconvenient or unexpected times.

Observe as Martha hears sounds outside her house and recognises the voice of Jesus. Conflicting emotions overtake her. Jesus is a friend whom she knows and likes greatly and on any other day she would be honoured and delighted if he decided to visit. But why has he chosen today of all days, when she finds herself incredibly busy?

As soon as Jesus enters the house he can sense her unease. Could it be that he picks up the same vibes when he comes to visit you? 'Go away and come back at a more opportune time' may be your signature tune also.

Just then, you notice your sister Mary entering the scene. Without apology, she finds a place beside Jesus and starts a conversation. You can feel a rush of envy and anger. Envy over her easy ability to just be with Jesus and anger over the way she has so lightly skipped out of her share of the housework and left everything to you. Somewhere deep down you are aware of feelings of resentment and sadness tugging you in two directions. Work calls, and you resent having been left with more than your fair share of it. You are sad too, because you recognise an opportunity to be present with and interact with Jesus.

So, moved by pique, you ask Jesus to intervene on your behalf and make your sister shoulder her share of the family responsibilities. You're rather surprised at his reply. Your sister has chosen the better part, you're told. You did not have to isolate yourself in the kitchen. No one forced you into that role. You could have carved out the time and stayed at his feet, but you didn't.

You decide to make a special prayer. 'Lord, help me to go slower and enjoy life. Help me not to be always running and not to always have a list of engagements that prevent me enjoying your presence. Teach me not to be a victim of my own compulsions. Help me to "do" less and to "be" more.'

When you are ready bring the meditation to a close.

Try the following as a short body exercise that might help you into meditation.

Settling yourself into a secure and peaceful position, take a few deep breaths and ask that you may be given energy and a sense of the presence of God.

As you exhale, focus on your neck and shoulders and try to notice whether there is any tension in those locations.

When you first begin to meditate (and for quite a long time afterwards) you will probably notice your thoughts beginning to jump around from one place to another shortly after you begin. (In India, they call this the 'monkey in the tree' mentality, for they know only too well that monkeys have a tendency to jump from branch to branch and chatter all the while.) That's the way our minds often feel as we settle into prayer.

As you pray, you may feel anxious, or bored, or confused or distracted. Just do your best to relax and quieten down.

Try to watch your mind at work and note your consciousness as it moves through the various emotions.

Don't judge yourself. Just note what's going on.

Trying to observe all that is happening will be difficult at first and you may well find that you are tempted to give up. Keep at it. Meditation takes time – and practice.

Recall the incident recounted in the gospel passage and try, in your imagination, to sketch in the two sisters and their goings-on the day Jesus arrived. Call to mind also the personalities of both Martha and

Mary. Imagine, if you can, Jesus approaching this house as the two sisters pursue their interests inside.

What have they been up to all day? Set the scene until Jesus finally comes knocking on their door.

Martha is the one we concentrate on first. She comes to the door, and there are a lot of good things about her that are obvious. She is a worker. She's in the right place at the appropriate time, but other cares compete for her attention. She wants to show off her place and to have her establishment in shipshape order. Not only was she not prepared to open herself to Jesus, but she was piqued and quite put out that somebody else might avail of the opportunity.

Now, apply the above scene to your own life. Begin to think of the times when you were too busy to notice his knock, or you weren't in great form, or perhaps felt that most of the work around the place was being dumped on you. When he came knocking you were busy, perhaps too busy, about many things and forgot about the one thing that was truly important.

So settle yourself for a few moments just thinking about those times. Maybe he was close by, trying to reveal himself? For the times when you mumbled and grumbled, ask forgiveness. Think of the second sister, Mary, who at times seemed to receive little response to her requests but had the courage to stick in there. 'She has chosen the better part.' Ask the Lord to help you do the same.

8

WHAT HAPPENS IF DARKNESS STARTS TO OVER-
COME THE LIGHT?

*Any fool can learn from his mistakes. The wise man learns from
the mistakes of others.*
Otto von Bismarck

We've been looking at the influence our parents or those who have
gone before us might have had on our lives. We've also been giving
thanks for the legacy their influence has bestowed. That's all very
well, but what if some of those early influences may have been less
than healthy?

I have a friend whose father had a favourite saying: 'Be very careful
when you choose your parents. It's likely to affect the rest of your
life.' This thought came to mind recently because I work with university students and each year we organise a sponsored walk with them.
The money collected is sent to a well-known charity that deals with
homeless young people in Ireland who have been messed about badly
in their youth. As we want to let the students know exactly what they
will be collecting for, we invite the founder of this charity to talk to
them about the project and its aims.

Last week we invited our guest speaker along and let him mix
freely with the students. He's a very practical, down-to-earth individual and usually gets straight to the point. He nearly always takes a
concrete situation from his workplace to explain the effects of home-
lessness and youth deprivation. This year, his story was about a par-

ticularly problematic individual from one of his hostels. It appears that the staff in that particular hostel has been going through a rough time recently because the individual in question has been causing mayhem among his peers. Whenever this fellow is asked to lend a hand with any unpleasant task, be it washing up, sweeping the floor or tidying a room, his reaction is always the same. If he doesn't like the task, he just lashes out and usually gives the one making the request a smack in the face! This, as you can imagine, brings all proceedings to a sudden halt. Obviously, staff do not find this conduct acceptable. They are used to dealing with highly unstable customers, but everybody has a limit.

Recently, the workforce arrived at our speaker's door (he is the director of the establishment) and explained that they had come to the end of their tether. Either the violent one would have to be shown the door or staff members would resign 'en bloc'. The director was in a bit of a quandary because the hostel's policy is very forgiving. Throwing a homeless youth out on his ear would go very much against the grain. All the same, he could hardly expect his team members to put up with such belligerence.

Great tact and discretion were called for. In short, the wisdom of Solomon would be needed to sort out this mess. How could an acceptable solution be achieved? For days the director pondered his predicament but no good solutions presented themselves. It looked as if the youth would have to go. On about the third day of this dilemma the director sat down for morning coffee. He was on his own in the hostel's dining room, but before long, who should appear but the violent resident. Upon invitation, he sat down and began to talk. It was not an easy conversation. The young man began by speaking about his home life and how his violent and disruptive father affected the atmosphere. It transpired that his dad drank far too much and whenever he appeared in the family home he was invariably drunk. Not alone that, but his opening salutation usually came in the form of an order that was roared out aggressively. This instruction demanded that his son tackle some piece of work straight away, and if the lad did not jump instantly to the task, his father immediately smacked him hard in the face. It was only as the boy got older that he worked out his best line of defence. As he put it himself, 'As soon as my father walked into the room I straight away made an attack on him before he could get a chance to bellow out his directives to me. I got my blows in first, and that, at least, gave me a fifty per cent chance of staying on my feet in the shenanigans that usually followed.' As soon as the director heard these words, he understood where the young man's disruptive actions sprang from. So, too, did the hostel staff team when they were told the story. They were able to talk to the lad and explain that there were other – and possibly better – ways of dealing with requests made of him. Since these conversations have taken place, calls for the removal of the adolescent have ceased and huge improvements in the overall situation have been achieved. The director ended his anecdote by saying that he was often struck by the fact that we have no choice when it comes to picking our parents. He himself could easily have had the lad's parents, while the troubled youth could have had his. It made the director extremely grateful for the parents given to him in the lottery of life.

That story left an indelible impression on me, so the very next day I proceeded to use it as sermon material at a Mass I was celebrating. Shortly after I finished, a lady came up and told me she was deeply touched by what she had just heard. She explained that she had attended her grandson's baptism the previous Sunday when just two newborns were due to be blessed. Alongside the 'apple of her eye', as she put it, a baby girl was also due for christening. As the lady delicately put it, the parish she was attending was very genteel and you would expect any child baptised there to come from a polite family. However the family opposite her that morning seemed anything but refined. In fact they looked wild and uncouth. She was determined not to judge by appearances, and took the opportunity at the end of the service to follow the other family down the aisle. The very young brother of the second baptised child – himself only about three years of age – was the very last one to make his exit. As they walked out side by side, this elderly woman leaned over and remarked to him how smart the young lad looked in his new sailor suit. 'He just looked at me in total bemusement as I made my remarks,' she said. 'I told him again how well the outfit looked on him and a hard stare came into his three-year-old face. Despite that setback, I made one last effort to establish friendly relations and repeated my admiration. It was a mistake. His face darkened and hardened as if a black cloud had passed over it. He brought his features very close up to mine and spat out, "F... Off".' As she ended her tale she added politely, 'I do apologise for my language but I don't really know any acceptable translation for that phrase, and all I can say is that some families make it almost impossible for a youngster to grow up as a reasonably decent human being because he could only have learnt that behaviour and language in the home and modelled it from his family setting.'

As we mentioned at the beginning, 'Be careful how you choose your parents'. If God did the choosing for you and you were greatly favoured by his choice, don't forget to pray and give thanks, however briefly, when you get down to your next bit of prayer.

I'm delighted if previous chapters have made you more aware of how grateful you should be for faith gifts bestowed on you by those who guided your early footsteps. However, it may be the case that memories or experiences from earlier years have not been so pleasant. We often meet people who are acutely aware of the terrible legacy they believe they have inherited. Influential figures from their past may have damaged them, or experiences they have either been subjected to or have had to work through may have left them traumatised.

What can a person do to lessen the impact such memories and reminiscences may have had on them? This is a hard one to answer, but quite recently I read a book by Karl Marlantes, an American who served as a marine in Vietnam. The book was called *What is it Like to Go to War?* and it had really good insights that might throw some light on the subject we are thinking about.

In 1969, at the age of twenty-three, Marlantes was dropped into the jungle in Vietnam and asked to command a platoon of forty or so men who would have to live or die by his decisions. What made the book interesting for me was the way the writer reflected – many years afterwards – on how that traumatic experience had left an indelible mark on him and his comrades later in life. None of them, I suppose, had given much thought to what effect the whole experience would have on their future conduct or character but this particular marine's unusual capacity to ruminate on and be philosophical about what he and his buddies went through makes for a captivating read. He notes that sometimes we find ourselves at a place in life where we don't want to be – in horrendous situations or teamed up with unsavoury companions. Marlantes reminisces about his tour of duty in Vietnam and concludes that much of his time there left a stain or scar both on him and on those he commanded that will, in all likelihood, never be removed. What he saw, and what he was forced to endure, was not healthy. That much he understood, but what he should do about it was much less clear to him. His reflective nature, and ability to stay with what was going on inside meant that the issue would not go away. Indeed, the question was made more real for him when he saw the destructive actions of some of his former buddies. He suspected, and with good reason, that the times and situations they had been through had also wrought havoc on them. For years this bothered him, for, as he said, 'I'd never been able to tell others what was going on inside me so I forced those images back, away. When I stayed with the goings-on inside, out came this overwhelming sadness.'

Marlantes noticed something else, however. When he managed to confront and stay with the demons inside rather than ignoring them or pushing them underground, healing followed. He thus thought it important that integrating the feelings of sadness, rage, helplessness and trepidation should not be something left to chance but should be built into the process of war. He strongly suspected that those who have been through harrowing events should be encouraged to talk about them and examine their legacy. He quotes John Mackie, his philosophy teacher at Oxford, who used to ask him why he assumed there was only one person inside him. He explained that psychoanalyst Carl Jung maintained that we all have a shadow side to our beings and that a part of us just loves maiming, killing and torturing. It's not, as you might suspect, a part whose existence we're keen to give much credence to, let alone accept. It's better, however, to be honest about its presence within us rather than blot out any mention of its existence. Recognising our shadow's existence gives us a chance to grapple with it and confront whatever shape it takes. When Marlantes looked not only at his own post-war history, but at the subsequent histories of those who had fought in Vietnam with him, he noted that the self-defeating activities of all of them had blighted not only their own lives but the lives of those around them. 'All of us know, at one level or another, how little we have fulfilled ourselves and how much of our potential has been left untrained and undeveloped.'

Shadow issues exist for many of us and are never easily defeated or overcome. Marlantes points out that being placed in intense war situations drives home this point to all combatants. The astute ones realise that they, and those around them, will have to live with the darkness as well as the light within themselves as soon as they return from the mayhem that is war. Certainly they will need to heal the body and the mind, but they will also need to heal the soul. How this is to be done is not easily explained. The dark parts of ourselves have to be challenged because it's hard to be at peace with yourself without first coming to terms with them. Trying to forgive yourself for past actions is part of this process. When you try to break the hold of evil that may have taken a firm grip, that trait of character or 'devil within' will fight back hard to reassert its authority. It will not, as scripture tells us, give up easily. Remember the gospel's cautionary words about being careful about trying to shoo out minor devils from your home because such 'devils' are likely to look for reinforcements and bring more powerful brothers or sisters along to retake their terrain. Being vigilant should help us to bring our better selves to the party and keep our less healthy characteristics at bay. It won't completely eradicate the latter but it may help to stop them bothering us beyond endurance.

We know that the sleazy or less wholesome practices of our past can be harmful to our prayer lives. We just have to hope that the good influence achieved by parents, grannies or other role models may counteract any damage done in the past. The strength their actions have built up in us allows us to take note of the effects of past misbehaviours and how these may have weakened us. I've often been struck by the observations of Dervla Murphy as she made her way through various foreign countries, trying to fathom what was going on in them. She had a terrific eye for detail and, on some of her more risky forays into war-torn lands, observed an unusual phenomenon. She had a 'nose' that seemed to pick up anything that brought on feelings of dread and foreboding. A sixth sense told her that something sinister was – or had been – afoot in the place she was visiting. It was only when she got home and began to research the area she was travelling through that she unearthed some particularly atrocious events that had happened at exactly the spot she felt intimidated by. It's as if, she said, the evil of the unspeakable deeds done there had somehow seeped into the soil and now, over time, are released as a sort of poisonous vapour back into the atmosphere. Evil leaves a mark. It's as if the darkness is trying to overcome the light.

So if you're worried that an event from your past may be having a detrimental effect on your spiritual life, you might take that very point to prayer. Likewise, if a character you interacted with in bygone times still seems to be dragging you down, it may be a good idea to share that with the Lord. Sometimes, there is no obvious solution to your slow progress and you may need to bring that very point of concern to Jesus. Just admit that you have no ready answer and hand it over. We try to let you, Lord, worry about any concerns we may have about the pace of progress we are making and we ask that your generosity may take over for a while and look after our dilemma.

Start by finding a quiet space and time and place yourself in God's presence.

It may help if you spell out in a single sentence or two what exactly you think the problem is. Getting the question right is a good first step.

Next, list the possible solutions to your problem. What steps forward are open to you? This may take time and at first nothing may come to mind. Persevere.

Jot down the advantages and disadvantages of each course of action you have come up with.

Remind yourself that God is a partner in this endeavour and may well inspire some ideas about how you might confront your problem.

Remind yourself that Jesus invited us to bring our worries and requests to the Father, so try not to hurry the Lord, or push too hard for an answer.

Some requests are answered in ways we do not expect, or less speedily than we might have wished, and sometimes the answer may be not to our liking.

An answer may not even come during the time of meditation but rather it may rise up through your unconscious mind on a later occasion when you are engaged in some other activity. It may leap from the pages of a book, or suddenly reveal itself in the words of a friend, or make its appearance in that halfway state between waking and sleeping late at night or early in the morning.

Pray that your inner mind might be unclogged so that God can get his answer through to you.

How do you know that the solution presenting itself is from God?

Well, St Ignatius, the founder of the Jesuits, used to say that sometimes a response is clear and unambiguous but more often it isn't. He also said that it's easier to see in retrospect whether the course of action we've taken has been for the best or not.

By engaging in this practice fairly regularly, you will increase your ability to see patterns and trends within yourself which have shown themselves in previous decision-making times. Insights gained in this way about how you react under pressure can be remarkably helpful in guiding you when fresh predicaments arise.

EXERCISE TWO: USING YOUR TALENTS (MT 25:14–30)

Introduction

Try to remember that when you are tense, worked-up, keyed-up or knotted-up your body realises it and puts your blood pressure up. Your breathing becomes irregular and your whole physical, mental and emotional being suffers. You need to wind down, calm down and settle down in order to relax and ponder what the Lord may be trying to say to you.

First, read the gospel story and prepare yourself for prayer.

Begin thinking about the three characters in the story. They have each been given talents. Look at the ways in which they use those gifts.

After some time, allow your imagination to place you in the gospel scene.

What talents do you think you have been given by God?
How have you used them?
Were you generous or mean in their use?
Could you have utilised your talents differently?
Do you think you might have other latent talents?
What are they?
Why have you not developed them?
Some people don't recognise their own talents – do you?

The character who was cursed in the story was not the one who had tried and had not been particularly successful. He was rewarded.

It was the one who had been too fearful to risk anything. That one was castigated.

Ask that your attitude be, 'I'd rather have tried and failed than not have tried at all.'

Some people have the great talent of developing the gifts of others. Can you remember such people in your own life?

Pray a prayer of thanks for them and ask for some of their generosity for yourself.

Have you drawn out the talents of those around you?

If you have, give thanks for that fact.

If you have not, ask that you may be a greater giver of encouragement in the future.

EXERCISE THREE: ALLOW YOUR BODY SENSATIONS TO HELP
YOUR PRAYER

Bring yourself to a quiet place and offer this time to the Lord.

See what state your body and mind are in at the moment.

If the focus of your attention shifts, be aware of the shift.

Talk silently to yourself: 'Now I am thinking ... Now I am irritated ... Now I am listening'.

Try to become aware of when you become distracted and, when you notice it happening, gently move the focus back to your basic object of attention.

Sharpen your awareness ... pick up the lightest sensations, sounds, touches of air passing through your nostrils.

Take only one small area of your body, such as a tiny spot in the centre of your forehead, and be aware of every sensation there.

If and when you experience silence, or a void, or emptiness, rest in it.

Now, withdraw in fantasy to any place where you have been happy. Take in every detail: sight, sound, smell, taste, touch. Notice what you feel.

Go in fantasy to any place that is likely to foster prayer ... seashore, mountain top, river bank, a silent church or the like. Do this in your memory or imagination and hear the sounds ... waves, wind, insects ... making your prayer in this context.

Withdraw in fantasy to any place where you had an intense experience of God and see the place as vividly as possible. Recapture the atmosphere. Relive the experience.

Many peak experiences in life would be very nourishing if we gave time to reliving them in a more leisurely fashion. Try to do this now.

Finish with the Lord's Prayer.

Choose a time and place and sit down.

Try to get your head, neck and chest in alignment.

Start by focusing on your heart area, somewhere close to the middle of your chest, and then, with your mouth closed, breathe in and out.

Keep your attention on that same central point as if you were using it to breathe in and out – and maintain a pace for your breathing that is slow, deep and regular.

Sometimes it helps to imagine that the room you are praying in is filled with a coloured mist – I find a yellow or golden tinge works best for me, but you can choose whatever colour best suits your mood. As you breathe in and out, try to imagine you are drawing this coloured mist deep within you. In a sense, you are drawing the breath or spirit of God into yourself and asking that it might infuse your being.

So, as you breathe, make a prayer and ask that the grace you are looking for may be given to you during this contemplative time. On each outbreath request that anything that may be blocking God's righteousness (such as tiredness, frustration, guilt, anger or pain) may be held at bay, at least for these few minutes.

Next, form a picture in your mind as you visualise this golden mist which is entering your being, and let the mist shape itself into tiny splinters of light like rays emanating from the Holy Spirit.

Now, slowly, allow the rays from the Holy Spirit to grow in size. With time, they will begin to fill you with goodness. Ask that the grace building up within you may begin to radiate outwards towards those you come into contact with today.

Send that blessing out ahead of you.

Ask that you may be a bringer of grace and goodness to those who are ill, lonely, afraid or without hope.

9

PROCRASTINATION

A land without a Lord is a dead land
Old Proverb

I have a friend who happens to be a priest, and he's very talented. That doesn't, however, save him from the Irish weather and he finds the long, damp winters difficult to cope with. They play havoc with his health, so a few years ago he talked over possible options with his bishop and the two of them decided that his wisest course of action might be to leave Ireland for a while and work in a parish abroad. As the bishop had a few powerful contacts overseas, he managed to get my friend linked up with a diocese on the West Coast of the United States. There, for the last ten years, my friend has been ministering in a parish and this novel arrangement is working out really well for him. His new parishioners are absolutely delighted by his Irish accent, which he lays on thick. The years have flown by and only recently did it strike him that he has been away for over ten years and has not once made the journey home to visit his nearest and dearest.

During the years away, a number of his immediate family have died and he realised that even more of them might not be around if he postponed a return visit much longer. This summer he finally bit the bullet and booked his passage. He was putting his bits and pieces into a suitcase when he came across a suit that he has hardly worn since he left these shores many moons ago. It still looked crisp and fresh. Even though he is not a snazzy dresser and does not worry about his image, he knew that there would be a lot of criticism in the small village he comes from if he turned up looking like a tramp. So the suit was in. As he packed the garment, he went through its pockets. Much to his surprise, he unearthed a cobbler's reclaim ticket neatly tucked away inside one of the pockets and vaguely remembered something from ten years ago that came back to his mind. He recalled that the very week he had departed for the United States, he had deposited a pair of shoes with the local cobbler and had promptly forgotten all about them. The reclaim docket he had found was the very one connected with those shoes.

Upon arrival in his native village he was amazed to find things very much as he had left them many years before. It's true that places looked a bit smaller than he remembered, but otherwise nothing much had changed. Even the old shoe shop was still in existence. Perhaps more surprisingly, the ancient cobbler whom he recalled from his youth and to whom he had given the shoes for repair was still in place and was hammering away at his usual resolute pace. I think it was at that moment that a whimsical thought came into my friend's mind. He's a 'character' and a bit of a joker, and so, putting his hand in his pocket to make sure the reclaim ticket was still in place, and keeping his face absolutely straight, he marched into the shop. Without so much as an explanatory comment, he put the ten-year-old docket on the counter before stepping back and waiting for a response. He didn't get the reaction he expected. There was silence for a moment, and then, very slowly, the old cobbler picked up the receipt and leisurely made his way to the back of the shop. It wasn't long before my friend began to hear mutterings and curses from the rear of the premises. These were low and indistinct at first and went on for a few minutes while the old man searched high and low among the dusty shelves. After two or three minutes of this pantomime, the proprietor reappeared from the dark recesses at the back of the store and – without the slightest trace of irony – handed back the reclaim ticket. 'They'll be ready next Friday,' was all he said.

When my friend regaled us with this story some time later, he remarked, firstly, that the cobbler was, in his opinion, a 'typical procrastinator' – which to you and me means somebody who is forever putting things on the long finger. He also mentioned that he himself was no mean judge of the breed. To illustrate this, he remembered how he had worked in an Irish retreat centre years ago and the fellow who looked after the financial affairs of the establishment was a bit of a dodderer. Whenever my friend needed something quickly, or required an up-to-date report on financial matters, the 'dodderer' never seemed to have figures to hand. One day, when things were even more chaotic that usual, and an accurate reckoning of how accounts stood was impossible to obtain, my friend exploded. He let out a few choice words about efficiency and then stormed out. All that evening, however, the incident preyed on his mind. He regretted deeply having lost his temper and couldn't get a wink of sleep. Finally he resolved to eat humble pie and say how sorry he was at the earliest possible opportunity. A suitable opening cropped up the very next morning and my friend was big enough to grab it. Even better, his apologies were accepted with the minimum of fuss. 'It was as well I did say how sorry I was,' he said later, 'because not long afterwards the old fellow dropped dead while out walking and I would never have forgiven myself or given myself a moment's peace if I had not made things up with him.'

We may find that we we're not shy in the 'procrastination' stakes ourselves. President John. F. Kennedy used to say that 'the time to be fixing your roof was while the sun is still shining and not when the rains have already begun to fall', so if you – like me – have a tendency to put things on the long finger, the above cautionary tale might be enough to shake you into productive activity.

Putting things off with regard to looking at how things stand between myself and God may be something worth considering while we still have the chance. This point was brought home to me recently when I heard a story about how Pope Francis was affected by a famous picture of Christ. It's by William Holman Hunt, an artist you may not be familiar with, but you might recognise one of his canvases if I describe it. This picture depicts a figure – presumably Jesus – standing outside an overgrown and long unopened door. The person knocking holds a lantern close to his face. The light from the lamp produces a wonderful glow which illuminates Christ's face. If this image is familiar, you may well have been particularly struck by the Christ figure. He's captured with his free hand raised high just before he knocks on the door. The image seems to suggest that Jesus is never far away from us and is constantly hoping to gain entry to any door that he comes upon.

When the picture was first produced, some eagle-eyed onlookers spotted what they thought was an error or oversight. I need hardly mention that they sprang into action and complained to the artist about the inconsistency. The picture appeared correct in most details but the illustrator seemed to have forgotten to include a door handle. When Holman Hunt was challenged about this, he explained to his critics that – as far as he was concerned – the absence of a handle was deliberate. To him, it added to the story, for it highlighted the fact that what was going on was an open invitation to us by Jesus to develop a mutual relationship. Nothing was being forced. Nothing demanded. We had a say in the proceedings. Before anything would begin from his side, we – for our part – would have to make use of the handle on our side of the door to make it possible for him to enter.

Hunt's picture came to my mind again recently as I was reading a book about the newly elected pontiff. It seems that shortly after Pope Benedict announced his intention to retire from the papacy, the wheels of papal succession began to move quickly. First, a date for the conclave to elect a new pope was decided upon. Next, the cardinals were summoned to Rome from all parts of the world and were asked to begin proceedings without delay. In order to prepare themselves adequately, the assembled group was given a few days together before voting actually began. The hope was that they would get to know each other as fully as possible. They would also have the opportunity to think about which world and Church issues seemed most important to them. Thus, they would be helped in their deliberations and in the choice they had to make.

To ensure that greater knowledge about each other was actually achieved, the whole assembly first met informally. During these days, each cardinal was allowed to make a five-minute presentation to the assembled group. It meant that everyone could say a little about themselves, where they came from, what issues and pressures were particularly relevant in their part of the world and what they felt might be the foremost of these that the new pontiff would need to address. As you might imagine, some of these presentations were fairly lively. Everybody knew that the Church, during the past twenty years or so, has faced enormous trials and tribulations. All of the cardinals said their piece and one of the last interventions at this initial stage was made by the cardinal from Buenos Aires, Jorge Bergoglio, a Jesuit from Argentina, and not the youngest of the cardinals by any means. Some already knew him quite well because he had been a major player in the previous conclave that had elected Pope Benedict. However, this time around his age seemed to suggest that he was unlikely to be a serious candidate. Be that as it may, his contribution was lucid and brief, and it made a deep impression on those who heard it.

One of those present, the Archbishop of Havana, Cardinal Jaime Ortega, was so taken by the address that he asked if he might have a copy of the text for his own private reflection. He was probably quite surprised when he was told by Cardinal Bergoglio that no such text existed. The future pope had spoken off the cuff to his brother cardinals and had simply put together his thoughts as they came to him. He did, however, agree to jot down notes about his reflections and promised to give them to the cardinal from Havana as soon as he could. When they arrived, they were quickly circulated to all, though the Argentine cardinal could hardly have anticipated the impact his words would have on future events. In his notes, Cardinal Bergoglio had taken an idea from the Book of the Apocalypse and from Holman

Hunt's picture in which we're asked to reflect on the fact that Jesus is never far away. He stands at the door of our experience and knocks. He is, as it were, 'outside' – but desires to come 'inwards'.

Cardinal Bergoglio, in the memo he sent to Cardinal Ortega, added something. Having first wondered whether the Church itself is too self-referential, he asked himself whether this trait might not restrict Christ's gifts. His question, in a sense, turned the usual conventional meaning of Hunt's picture on its head. Normally, we think that Jesus taps on the door because he wants to 'get in'. What, the future Pope Francis wondered, might be the scenario if the Lord actually desires to do exactly the opposite? What if he is knocking because he wants to get out! I find it invigorating to ask myself, 'Get out where? To do what?'

Our habits and practices – both individually and as a Church – may confine and ensnare Jesus. By being too 'precious', we – as individuals or Church – may restrict his life-giving grace and Spirit. As 'Church', we may be so self-referential that we confine Jesus within the institutionalised structure and smother his energising presence. Boris Pasternak, the Russian writer, used to say that God is never far away and is constantly looking for ways to speak to us. He's persistently 'knocking at our doors'. The way he put it is that 'when a great moment knocks on the door of your life it is often no louder than the beating of your heart ... and it is very easy to miss it'.

So take that as your task for the month. Ask yourself how best you might unfetter Christ's 'spirit' and allow it to play the part it wants in your spiritual rejuvenation.

First, choose a time and place and sit down.

Try to get your head, neck and chest in alignment.

Start by focusing on your heart area, somewhere close to the middle of your chest, and then, with your mouth closed, breathe in and out.

Keep your attention on that same central point as if you were using it to breathe in and out, and maintain a pace for your breathing that is slow, deep and regular.

Sometimes it helps to imagine that the room you are praying in is filled with a coloured mist – I find a yellow or golden tinge works best for me, but you can choose whatever colour best suits your mood. As you breathe in and out, try to imagine you are drawing this coloured mist deep within you. In a sense, you are drawing the breath or spirit of God into yourself and asking that it might infuse your being.

So, as you breathe, make a prayer and ask that the grace you are looking for may be given to you during this contemplative time. On each outbreath request that anything that may be blocking God's grace (such as tiredness, frustration, guilt, anger or pain) may be held at bay, at least for these few minutes.

Next, form a picture in your mind as you visualise this mist which is entering your being. Let the mist you see in your mind's eye shape itself into a tiny being, about the size of your thumb. Allow this silhouette to settle in the centre of your chest, close to your heart – and soon this small, thumb-sized form takes on a life of its own. In your imagination, see it begin to radiate light and peace to those it touches.

Now, slowly, allow this tiny being to grow in size. With time, it will begin to fill you with its presence and, as it does, try to experience your own body growing to contain it. Bestow on each object you want to pray for a sense of compassion and feel the coloured haze pour out from your being. Ask that the grace radiating from you may bring wholeness to all that you are coming into contact with.

After a few minutes, begin to see this substantial being you have become return to its original size. Stop here for a moment.

Reach down and, with your imagination, very gently place your hand on the head of this being. Bestow upon it your blessing. Experience simultaneously that which blesses and that which is being blessed. Send that blessing out to those who are ill, lonely, afraid or without hope. Allow the radiant being within you to assume its diminutive form, again becoming the size of a thumb. See it again in the middle of your chest, radiant with light and goodness. This is your inner guru. This is the being within you whom you meet when you go beyond your normal inner boundaries. When you wish, you need only sit and calm your mind and you will hear this being guiding you home.

Each morning, take a holy book and work with a thought. Don't read many pages. Just take one thought and sit with it for ten or fifteen minutes. Allow that thought to stay with you and deepen throughout the day.

EXERCISE TWO: JESUS WITH THOMAS (JN 20:19–31)

'On the evening of that day, the first day of the week, the doors being shut where the disciples were, for fear of the Jews, Jesus came and stood among them and said to them, "Peace be with you."

He showed them his hands and his feet.

Thomas was not with them so when he returned they told him they had seen the Lord – but he did not believe them.

Some days later, when the disciples were again together – but this time they had Thomas with them – Jesus re-appeared and said to the doubter, "Put your finger here and see my hands... do not be faithless, but believing."'

Note how the group were visited while they were at their lowest ebb. That's when Jesus chose to made his appearance.

When He was least expected ... and almost unrecognisable.

Your message, Lord, was simple ... 'Peace' ... and 'Have courage'. Now imagine yourself in Thomas's shoes. Think of the phrases he might have used.

'I wasn't there the first time when all the excitement took place.'

'Typical. I'm never there for the best bits.'

'So I didn't see, and therefore didn't believe.'

'Why should I have had faith? Would you have believed their tales?'

'They had undergone a personal experience. I was never given that opportunity.'

'I wasn't there and didn't see for myself and so can't believe, won't believe, don't believe.'

What would you have said if you were in Thomas's place?

But Jesus said, 'You believe, Thomas, because you can see. Blessed are those who don't see and still believe.'

Could those be his words to me also?

Those around Thomas tried to encourage his belief. You also may be aided in your belief by the people around you.

They may have seen Jesus, in different ways, and they may be trying to bring a sense of Christ's presence to you.

But you have to do something yourself. What did Thomas do? At least when he did see, he didn't continue to block out the truth. He didn't allow his embarrassment or his doubt to shut him off from Jesus.

Pray to Thomas for yourself, asking him that in your doubt he will now be the one to be a bringer of Christ to you.

A fair amount of our time in the noviceship was spent trying to learn how to pray. Each evening, a second-year novice (they were supposed to know something about how meditation might be attempted) selected a gospel passage for us and helped us look at how we might attempt to use the material the following morning.

After selecting and reading through the text (often the gospel to be read at the following day's Mass was chosen), our second-year 'expert' usually settled on five points that he thought might prove profitable. This system had the benefit of being clear and concise. Whether it was effective or not is another matter. Try it for yourself and see what you think.

Bring yourself to a place of prayer and settle down. You might kneel, or stand or sit (although as our noviceship prayer was always practised very early in the morning sitting down was dangerous). Remember that Jesus is present in this place, so ask for assistance if your attention begins to drift away from the task you have set yourself. When you feel settled, read the text you have chosen. We will assume for a moment that you have selected the passage about the storm at sea. If you are praying about Jesus and his disciples caught in a storm on the Sea of Galilee, you would try to imagine yourself with the disciples. They – and you – have had a hard day working with Jesus in one of the local towns and, as the day draws to a close, Jesus gets into the boat and suggests a little time for quiet relaxation. He is worn out from the labours of the day and drops off to sleep almost as soon as the trip begins. Start the first point in your imagination.

You sit right in the middle of the boat, taking in as much as you can of what is going on around you. What do you see? How many disciples are on board? What sort of expressions do they have on their faces? How rough is the sea? What do you hear, smell, notice, feel, taste? The answers to the these questions depend on how you are in your every-day life at present and what stresses and strains are affecting you.

What's going on in your life? That dictates which elements of the gospel narrative are going to leave the heaviest imprint. Get yourself into a reflective mood and allow the surroundings to help you to review what has been going on. Take a little time as you try to notice what reactions are making themselves felt.

Gradually, you begin to notice the atmosphere changing around you. The weather has got colder and the wind has picked up. Though Jesus is still asleep, your other companions definitely are not. As seasoned fishermen they are fully aware that your whole group is in peril. Only Jesus – still apparently comatose – seems oblivious to the danger. Each individual must decide what best to do... act now, or become paralysed by fear. The others throw the responsibility over to you and you shake Jesus by the shoulder. In his own good time, he responds.

Listen to his words. 'O you of little faith – why did you doubt?'

Let those words stay with you and see what profit they may bring.

EXERCISE FOUR: HEADING FOR THE BASEMENT (FANTASY PRAYER)

Carl Jung used to say that people in the west have lost the ability to meet God through myths and symbols. Because of this, we have impaired our ability to listen in silent contemplation to the voices within us. In olden times these intimate voices acted as wise guides, but nowadays they tend to do so less and less.

Go to your usual prayer place and allow yourself to breathe slowly and deeply.

Imagine that each breath is going down into your stomach, so that you are breathing with the stomach, rather than with the chest.

As you draw the breath deep into the pit of your stomach in a slow, relaxed manner you notice that this is producing a feeling of calm, because the pattern is steady and even. This method encourages a sense of calm and equilibrium.

During the breathing exercises, and indeed during the meditations themselves, you may very well find distractions creeping in. Don't let that deter you. Most people starting out, and indeed quite a few of the mystics, found themselves beset by difficulties of a similar type. Don't let that put you off – stay in the present.

If distracted, become aware of that fact, record it in your mind and note how it feels, and then return to the business at hand.

You may even be capable of befriending the distractions as they could have something to teach you. Such insights can assist interior transformation and this is no small thing – interior growth is one of the principal reasons why you have come to meditation in the first place.

Now commence the exercise by talking to yourself quietly, reminding yourself where you are and what you hope to do. Build up a rhythm in your breathing pattern by silently coaching yourself with a phrase, such as 'Breathing deeply in, two, three, four ... breathing softly out, two, three, four', or 'Breathing Christ in, breathing worry out' to heighten your awareness that Jesus is not far away.

Now imagine that you are in a tall building and use your imagination to picture yourself stepping into the elevator. As the doors close, push the button to take you down to the basement.

As the lift goes downwards, visualise yourself descending deeper and deeper into your inner self. Sometimes it helps to count off the floors as you descend, telling yourself all the while that you are becoming more and more serene. What you are hoping to achieve is a serene space within you where God and yourself might meet. Boris Pasternak used to say that when a great moment knocks on the door of your heart – in other words, when God is trying to speak to you – 'the sound is often no louder than the beating of your heart, and it's very easy to miss it'. Stay in that space and ask the Lord to help you be receptive to anything he might want to impart.

When you feel ready, imagine you are slowly getting back into the elevator and pushing the up button. As you ascend, notice that you are slowly coming out of the deep interior space and returning to the here and now.

When you finish, sit quietly for several moments with your eyes still closed, before gently allowing them to open and become accustomed to the light.

A friend of mine recently visited a meditation centre by the ocean where the presenter had those making the retreat seat themselves beside the sea. As they gazed out at the waves he offered the following meditation.

Start with the usual preliminaries.

When you feel suitably settled, picture yourself seated with the group.

It was early morning so the sun was just rising and the warmth of its rays began to spread over your face. Feel them on your face.

Use your senses and dare to believe that what you are seeing and feeling is real. Hear the waves as they come into shore, smell the sea, feel the gentle breeze as it softly caresses your face, with perhaps the occasional sounds of a bird's cry reaching your ears.

Try to stay with the beauty and the peacefulness of the moment.

Now try, in your imagination, to believe that the sea is beckoning you to walk towards it and towards the warmth of the sun.

Try to have some of St Peter's enthusiasm as you move towards the water. Even though you may feel foolish try to avail of the offer being made to you.

As you get to the water's edge, notice how the sun seems to be beckoning you nearer with its warmth.

As you start to walk towards it across the water, the sun seems to shimmer and encourage your progress.

When you get close, it bursts open to reveal the most unbelievable heart! It's as if God is drawing you close to himself and warming you by the grace of his love.

Stay with the warmth of that love for as long as you feel able.

When you are ready, let your awareness settle on the quiet sound of your breath moving slowly inwards and outwards, and thank God for the time you have been able to spend here.

10

STORM CLOUDS GATHERING

The suicide doesn't go alone, he takes everybody with him.
William Maxwell

I had to attend a funeral last week. It was in the West of Ireland and it was a horrible experience. As we entered the church, you could tell at once that nothing was as it should be. The family was there, heartbroken, not knowing where to put themselves. Their daughter of twenty-one, lying before them in her coffin, had taken her own life. As you might expect in a small rural village, the entire community had turned up, but you could tell that they were completely overwhelmed by the devastation they were witnessing around them and didn't know what to say or do. The local priests were outstanding and the first thing that struck me was that there were so many of them on the altar. Clergy from miles around seemed to be in attendance and I knew they must have gone to considerable trouble to find substitutes at short notice to look after their own parishes. Afterwards I asked one of them – the parish priest of a neighbouring parish – why he felt he had to be there. 'Ah, you'd always want to be with people at a time like this,' he said, and when I asked whether a catastrophe such as the one we were witnessing didn't tear the heart out of him, his reply was succinct. 'This is my third such funeral this week,' he said. 'In fact it's my third youth suicide, and unless people have something strong to hold on to in heartbreaking moments like this, it's easy enough to go under and be sucked into the black pit of despair.'

Nobody wants to think or talk about tragic deaths, particularly when they concern the young, but sometimes the culture around us forces us to at least mull over what such events do to us and our society. That thought occurred to me recently when Margaret Atwood, the award-winning Canadian writer, came and spoke to staff and students at my university in Ireland. One of her sentences, which has stayed with me, was 'some things need to be said, and said, and said again, until they don't need to be said any more', and that's the way I've felt about the subject of suicide for some time now. It's happening more and more in the circles that I frequent and I've had to grapple with the aftermath more often than I would like – and more than I suspect is healthy – in recent times. Let me explain.

As a university chaplain, I have been involved in numbers of funerals for those who have taken their own lives. All have been tough experiences. Each memorial service I've prepared took something out of me. Exactly how much I was never sure. I did get a little inkling of how much they impact on one when some weeks ago I sat with friends who are both wise and observant. Basically, we were trying to look at the effect our duties and work have on our mental and spiritual health. That's never easy, but it's always worth while.

Each member of the group took their turn to speak. First item on my agenda were those funerals I talked about earlier and had officiated at. I started out by recounting how the services had been formatted. Usually a few people who were very close to the deceased came together, I joined them, and as a group we tried to organise something that might be meaningful and provide a modicum of hope to those left behind. After I had been speaking for a couple of minutes, one of my companions gently asked how I was feeling. 'Not bad. These things happen and you have to deal with them as well as you can,' was all I could say and continued to talk. A few minutes later, the same observer again asked how I felt. 'Reasonably well, all things considered,' was my reply this time around. It took four or five interventions on my friend's part – always asking how I was feeling and how I had been bearing up over the last few weeks – before something began to register. My face went red. Anyone standing and observing the scene would have instantly recognised that I was pretty steamed up. My companions had seen it and one of them was gently trying to point out the obvious, but I myself had failed to notice what was going on or what damage had been done to me because of the memorial services. It was evident that the bereaved families had gone through a living nightmare. They had been forced to face all sorts of horrendous feelings – guilt, sorrow, distress and confusion, to name just a few – and I knew they must have been shaken to the core of their beings. The fact that I had also been traumatised seemed to have gone over my head – probably because I considered that any difficulties I had encountered were minimal in comparison to what the immediate families had been forced to endure. They were the ones who had suffered the shattering loss. They also were the ones who had to live with the terrible consequences.

Alongside the agonies mentioned above, those who remain behind in the suicide scenarios are often left with unanswered questions. At least that has almost always been my experience. In their desperation, thoughts such as 'Why?'and 'If only' are often on their minds as they search for ways they could have handled the lead-up events differently. Why had they not noticed the deceased's moods? Why had they left their loved one alone? If only they had caught the various little references to pain and despair in the preceding months they might have been able to prevent the catastrophe. Perhaps they had asked too much of their child by letting him leave home or had not listened carefully enough to what was being said on his visits home.

One question tumbles over another. The time, however, for being able to do anything positive has passed. It's hard to forgive oneself, to not heap blame on one's own shoulders, and understand that a person with suicidal tendencies usually – in so far as we can tell – chooses their time and place carefully. They do the deed in a way that guarantees that family members or concerned friends will be unable to intervene.

As our group talked about the tragic deaths we had been involved with and the resultant mayhem inflicted on all concerned, I was more than aware how badly and how horribly the bereaved families had been affected. Relatively speaking, I had suffered little, but it seemed to me that I was belly-aching and feeling resentful about being drawn in to the scenario. My worst side was coming into play and I wondered – as did my companions – why I was feeling so demoralised and hard done by. Something was going on, and it was not something I was very proud or happy about.

As we pondered and prayed over the puzzle, some insights began to emerge. Put simply, I'd thought that the people whose deaths we had to remember were – in all cases – young, talented and bursting with potential. To all outward appearances, they were successful, healthy and financially secure. What possible reason, then, could they have for killing themselves? That's about as far as my understanding went. My feelings of frustration and gloom were probably added to by factors that I'm embarrassed to mention and which probably seem trivial in the extreme. The tragic deaths I'm talking about tend to take place without any warning, at the most inopportune time, in the most inaccessible places, and when one is very busy. You are shattered by the news, have to drop everything, and get down straight away to the memorial planning. Much of the above sounds – and probably is – egotistical and selfish. It also includes, on my part, many misconceptions and downright inaccuracies about suicide. For instance, the first notion I may have to put right is that suicide is nothing more than an act of despair. I have a mental picture in my head of Judas Iscariot in his darkest moments. I see Judas with a never-ending life of remorse stretching ahead and so, in my thinking, he slumps into despondency. This may be true, but modern research seems to suggest that the act of taking one's own life is most likely to happen as a result of illness. Just as the body at times cannot handle some weaknesses successfully, so too the spirit or soul may find itself confronted by deadly wounds that seem impossible to overcome. Far from being an act of free will, it often appears as if the sufferer's last act is a desperate attempt to end unendurable agony. A reasonable comparison might be to think about those caught in New York's Twin Towers catastrophe who burst their way out through the uppermost windows as the flames approached. That seems more like an act of desperation than an act of despair. Their motive, one suspects, was escape, not self-destruction – which leads me to ask whether we can have any idea what is going on in the tortured minds of those who contemplate self-harm in the days and weeks leading up to their tragic demise.

From the stories I have encountered, it seems as if the young people involved in the heartbreaking deaths were not acting in any sort of rational way when they took their lives. They were in no mental condition to take into account the legacy they were leaving behind or to consider the likely impact of their actions on those close to them. Given that scenario, we need to rethink the notion that suicide puts a person outside the mercy of God. Remember that after the resurrection, when the apostles were in the grip of desolation and despair, Christ went through locked doors to breathe forgiveness and hope upon them. He knew they were unable to function normally or to open themselves either to new life or to hope. Trepidation and hopelessness had paralysed them. Is it not reasonable to assume, then, that Jesus might be equally generous to those who feel themselves to be in intolerable situations? I suspect our wounded ones who fall victim to suicidal thoughts and actions are far more likely to receive a listening and sympathetic reception from Christ than they are from today's culture. I found some comments from A. S. Byatt, in her story 'The Chinese Lobster', helpful here. She mentions that if those contemplating their own deaths could imagine the terror and the pain caused to those who remain after a suicide, they would not be able to carry out the act they are considering. She also notes that when one is at such a desolate point in one's life, it's hard for the sufferer to imagine the wreckage left behind because everything seems clean, clear and simple. There remains only one possible course of action. Byatt concludes by saying that speaking about suicide in general terms is difficult because each individual's death is his or her own and is intensely private, unknowable and terrible. Suicide will have seemed to its perpetrator to be the last and best solution out of a number of terrible options.

As our group tried to mull over the effects that these youthful deaths were having on their immediate families – and on those conducting the memorial services – some reflections stayed with us. We noted that each suicide is different, intensely private, unknowable and terrible. While those taking their own lives are making a choice, they may not even remotely grasp the fact that they don't go alone. In a way they take everybody with them. None of us in that group could rid ourselves of the images of desolation, confusion and guilt that we had seen on the faces of the parents, colleagues, children and friends left behind. As one family member said to me, 'When my sister killed herself she killed many of the best memories I had of her, for it's as if she was saying to me that I never really knew her.' Each of our group agreed that dealing with tragedy takes everybody's energy away. We had all recognised the fact that everyone touched by tragedy needs, in one way or another, to forgive themselves for their real or imaginary failings. One member, who had worked in London as a hospital chaplain, said that on her very first evening four or five patients died and as she sat by the bed of another who was not far from death, she was startled by his question. 'Do you think God will ever forgive me my sins?' His query, as she readily admitted, had her nonplussed. Afterwards, she asked a more experienced associate what her best response might have been and was told that the co-worker would have sat by the patient's bed and just held his hand. 'I would have let him talk,' her colleague said, 'because time after time I have been amazed at how people, if a space is opened up for them, can get deep down to what is really going on within and thus reach surprising spiritual depth, even when they think they don't have any spiritual beliefs left. Everybody has their own spiritual wisdom, and when you let people talk you allow this life wisdom come to the surface.'

Members of our group started to realise more and more that if we ourselves, or the people we are working with, are thrown into really difficult life situations, those experiences need to be faced and worked through. They say that during the liberation of the Nazi concentration camps during the Second World War, the prisoners, who had gone through a nightmarish experience, emerged hesitantly and slowly from their barracks. The liberating forces noticed that they blinked a couple of times and then walked timidly and slowly into their compounds. Afterwards, their liberators realised that what the prisoners had gone through was the only life they had known for an age. The terror of thinking for yourself, acting for yourself, deciding for yourself and accepting the consequences of your own decisions was more than they could handle. They couldn't act like free human beings straight away.

But even in terrible situations like the concentration camps, people who look to move the situation on in a positive fashion can extract good. You may remember the name Paul Rusesabagina, who famously ran the hotel in Africa known popularly as the Hotel Rwanda. He found himself placed in an impossible situation during those terrible times of savagery and mayhem between the warring tribes of Hutus and Tutsis. Through his calmness and wise judgements he managed to build a place of calm in his hotel because he had the unique ability, even in extreme circumstances when people were hacking each other to death around him, to extract serenity from the depths of the madness. When asked how he managed to hold things together and keep his head above water, he explained that in his youth his philosophy was pretty simple He felt that people were either good or bad, black or white. As he got older he began to realise that people were not so easily defined. They were fairly complex, and able to maintain two attitudes in their minds at once. The way he put it was that people have a soft side and a hard side. Neither is in absolute control. During that time of turmoil, his hotel was often used as a place of refuge by those trying to flee the anarchy and he found he had to negotiate with crooks of all descriptions on the victims' behalf. His basic belief that nobody was all black or all white, all good or all bad, stood him in good stead on such occasions. He tried to imagine that the aggressors were both soft and hard, and it was the soft side he had to try to locate within them. If he could get his fingers into their soft side, the advantage was his. He could, in a sense, transform them by colouring the atmosphere of their meeting and it surprised him that this was true not just for a few of those he had to negotiate with, but with almost all. So the way we approach a situation – the antagonism or composure we bring to the table, so to speak – can radically alter the outcome.

In Ireland, they tell a story about a man driving his car furiously into a rural petrol station and demanding rudely of the aged custodian that he get a move on with filling the tank. As the owner goes deliberately about his task, the visitor aggressively asks what the natives are like around this area. In response, the old man asks him where he has just come from and, on being told, inquires how the car driver found the people in that locale. 'They were thick, and slow and ignorant.' As soon as he's told that, the owner simply says, 'That's the way you'll find them here too.' You have to listen closely to the words used, as the old man chose them with great precision. He was not suggesting that his neighbours were in any way deficient. Rather, what he implied was that the car driver was likely to find a mirror image of himself wherever he travelled. The message you give out, I'm afraid, is likely to be the one you will receive back.

To sum up, any sort of bereavement creates stress, but trying to work with families who have lost loved ones in tragic circumstances piles on extra pressure which needs to be acknowledged and faced. How the ritual of the memorial service is carried out is a good deal more important than what is said. Years ago, deaths of all sorts in Ireland – and particularly heart-rending deaths – evoked a practice known as an 'Irish wake'. This provided all sorts of helpful assistance for those who had lost loved ones. At wakes, you could cry or laugh, be silent, or talk as much as you wanted. There were old women present who were almost professional 'criers', and they acted as a sort of framework of support. Their presence held you together during your darkest hours and provided a path back into normal living when you felt ready. Because culture has changed so much and so quickly, a lot of ancient wisdom regarding what is needed around times of deep loss has been taken away from us. We no longer want to stay with the pain but would rather use – and society would rather give – a pill to deal with our difficulties. Whether that really deals with the dilemma, or cloaks it by inducing a coma-like state, is debatable, for it seems likely that the coma-inducing pill postpones the pain but probably makes it break out in a more damaging way at a later point in life.

If you keep a journal or diary, reflect on the contents during your meditation time. You may well be surprised at what it can teach you. This point was brought home to me over the past year as I listened to an Irish radio programme about sexual abuse. As my heart sank, I started to think about what such programmes and newspaper articles had being doing to my spirit. I let my mind wander back over some of the issues and pressures that had been floating to the surface of my awareness over recent months to see if the insights that come to mind might bring a better sense of balance and peace to my heart and soul.

I began to think about the programme I had been listening to. How was that programme making me feel? I knew it was somehow dragging me down, but why?

I knew I had turned the programme off with a feeling of disgust and wondered why. I began to realise that the disgust was connected with horror/denial/shame on my part.

How could these actions be perpetrated by priests, sisters and members of religious orders who were supposed to have entered religious life with the highest ideals?

Part of my anger, I suspected, was because I knew that the institutional Church – of which I am a part – had not defended the innocent, and that many of those who had made complaints were telling the truth. I have to speak in public on Christ's behalf, but how can one defend the indefensible?

People are angry and it took the media to disclose the truth, not the Church.

I have often wondered what a barrister feels like when he is being asked to defend someone he does not believe in. It begins to dawn on me that something of that feeling may be with me now.

So I wonder how best I might work with some of those feelings and, finally, I ask some members of the congregation if they have any wise words to utter about my dilemma.

'Why not go back to the scriptures?' they suggest, for Jesus said, 'Bring the children to me.' Their innocence and beauty should bring hope and encouragement, not shame and despair.

So today perhaps we might pray for two things. Firstly, that you do not sink into gloom and walk away from Jesus because some of his followers let their worst selves come to the surface. Secondly, that those who were courageous enough to report what had happened to them, who grieved for their innocence and who had to endure the horror, will be given a sense of God's goodness to assist them through their ordeals.

Begin your meditation in the usual way by engaging in one of the breathing exercises. As you breathe in, ask that Jesus grants you quietness and serenity during your time of prayer. As you breathe out, try to let go of anything that might be disturbing the mellowness you seek. Allow your breath to flow at its own pace and intensity, fast or slow, and continue to ask for the equanimity you require.

Open your bible at the gospel of Luke (12:5).

'Now there was a man full of leprosy in one of the towns where he was; and when he saw Jesus, he fell prostrate, pleaded with him, and said, 'Lord, if you wish, you can make me clean.' Jesus stretched out his hand, touched him, and said, 'I will do it. Be made clean.' And the leprosy left him immediately'.

Now try to imagine yourself in the sick man's position.

For years you have seen your physical condition get worse.

You have neither the money nor the contacts to change your situation.

In fact, far from getting better, your situation has gradually got more and more desperate.

Your family, who up to now have been sympathetic and supportive, have been forced by public opinion to insist that you move away from home.

The local community cannot take the risk of being contaminated.

So in these past weeks you took the few bits and pieces you possessed and brought them well outside the city limits. Others with a similar condition to yours have set up a sort of wretched township out here.

Each day has been a living nightmare. Now you have to contend not only with your illness, but with loneliness and rejection as well.

Everyone in this pitiable setting has to fend for themselves. Trying to break through the barriers of fear and rejection is almost impossible.

Very little gives a person hope here but today something monumental has happened. It's rumoured that Jesus is in the vicinity.

Take your courage in your hands and see if you can get close to him.

Paint the picture for yourself. Are others from the leper community also trying to avail of this opportunity?

Have they also heard that Jesus might be about?

Do they have the courage and tenacity required to find him?

Are they prepared to put up with the rebuffs and complaints they are likely to endure for showing themselves in a public place?

Will they get to their destination before you?

Will they be the first to make a plea for mercy?

Is there any way you can give your chances a little boost?

And then you see a crowd ahead of you. No matter how reluctant you are, or how ashamed, you must get over there.

Does the crowd try to eject you or open up to make a pathway towards Jesus?

Stay with the scene and see what happens next.

Finally, hear the words that Jesus speaks to you. 'Of course I want to heal you.'

Give thanks and bring the meditation to a close.

Read the story and notice the events that unfold. They may be able to teach us something about how we ourselves interact with Jesus.

Watch how Jesus comes into contact with Bartimaeus. The blind man lives in a world of his own, a dark world, cut off from those around him. Thought he cannot see in the conventional sense, perhaps he has a power of sight that we know very little about. He has certainly grasped the fact that Jesus is out of the ordinary, that he has extraordinary powers and great generosity towards those in trouble. Well, Bartimaeus is in trouble and he is not afraid to let others know that.

At the very beginning of the gospel story, Bartimaeus puts one part of his persona and his courage on display. As so often happens in the gospel stories, a moment of opportunity has come the way of one particular individual and he – for one – is not going to let the chance of something truly breathtaking pass him by.

He seizes the moment. He takes the initiative, though others may try to restrain him and stand in his way. He refuses to be cowed. This might be his only opportunity and so he shouts out with great gusto towards Jesus and the assembly. Despite the fact that many tell him to be quiet, his intervention brings the crowd to a halt. In a way, all those people who shout at the blind man and try to deter him represent those who attempt to stand in our way when we think about changing. They are like those who, in their hopelessness and despair, tell us not even to go on trying when the going feels rough.

The Indian poet Tagore writes that the song he wanted to sing has never happened because he has spent his days stringing and unstringing his instrument. Whenever I think about these lines, I notice how the busyness of my days and nights makes it difficult to catch glimpses of God in any quiet spaces that come my way. I get so caught up with my schedule and with the hurry and worry of life that I miss the song of goodness that is waiting to be sung through me. Jesus doesn't allow the constant whirl of activity going on around him to distract him from attentiveness. It's important not to waste our time, but it's equally important at times to be still and savour the goodness of God around us.

Bartimaeus believes in Jesus' power and refuses to let the crowd stifle his enthusiasm. As soon as Jesus points a way forward and asks the blind man what exactly it is he wishes for, Bartimaeus is ready. So should we be ready because that same question, 'What exactly is it that you are looking for?' is one Jesus often uses in his encounters with people. He does not presume to know exactly what the person is looking for. This is wonderful because we are often a bit hazy about what exactly it is that we require.

Encounters with the divine often engender fear.

Let's see what Our Lady can teach us from such an encounter.

'In the sixth month, the angel Gabriel was sent from God to a city of Galilee named Nazareth, to a virgin betrothed to a man whose name was Joseph, of the house of David; and the virgin's name was Mary. And he came to her and said, "Hail, O favoured one, the Lord is with you!" But she was greatly troubled at the saying, and considered in her mind what sort of greeting this might be. And the angel said to her, "Do not be afraid, Mary, for you have found favour with God. And behold, you will conceive in your womb and bear a son, and you shall call his name Jesus'."

Place yourself with Our Lady during one of her moments of confusion.

For Mary, the visit of the angel is a frightening and confusing moment but also a time of opportunity.

Do such times of opportunity in your own life also seem threatening?

Note how the initiative of the offer lies entirely with God.

God begins the conversation with Mary, as he does with us, breaking into our lives in unexpected ways.

The angel Gabriel helps Mary discern. She is free to choose either to accept or reject the proposal made to her.

Looking back at the event, can you now see God's hand in the proceedings?

Mary says 'yes' to a future she does not know. Her generosity and courage are boundless. The modern mind may have difficulty believing in the miraculous, but such belief lies at the very heart of the gospels.

Spend a little time going back over happenings in your own life during the past year. Might it be possible that God has been suggesting possibilities to you for consideration?

Have you even noticed these suggestions?

Might they hold the seeds of growth for your own faith life?

11

THE LION KING

Why not go out on a limb – that's where all the fruit is.
Mark Twain

I've recently begun to work in a Dublin parish and one of the tasks you find yourself taking on is looking after funeral liturgies. Being a new arrival, you're faced with a disadvantage here. You don't know very much about the people you are being asked to bury and you know you are going to need a good deal of local help. First, you try to talk with members of the bereaved family. This helps, as it allows you to fill in some of the background and assists you in finding out what the deceased person was really like. You know you are going to have to console those left behind and say some complimentary words about the deceased, but speaking about the virtues of the recently departed when you know very little about them seems a bit insincere. I often ask if a family member will speak during the ceremony and give some input on what they remember about their loved one. Usually this works pretty well, and a son or daughter or family friend is more than happy to oblige. Occasionally, though, this approach encounters a stumbling block and the whole enterprise comes to an abrupt halt.

This was the case last week when I knocked on a newly bereaved family's door. The elderly lady who had just died had two daughters and both were reserved and shy. Neither wanted to stand up at the memorial service because – for them – the idea of getting to their feet in front of the congregation seemed like a fate worst than death. They both declined and said they would much prefer if I did the talking – which seemed fair, but still left me in a predicament because I really knew very little about their mother's life history or about her strengths and interests. I told them I would be greatly helped if they could share with me a few of their most vibrant memories and reminisces. Both daughters had claimed to be at least as shy as their mother and they proved true to their word, for during our conversation together neither of them offered any anecdotes. All they would say was that their mother was an absolute lady, being both reserved and dignified. I already had my hand on the latch when suddenly the older daughter remembered one particular story that the old lady often told her grandchildren, which was a bit out of the ordinary.

It seems that their recently deceased granny had come to Dublin from an isolated part of the country many moons ago and had conceived her eldest daughter in the first year of her marriage. To build up local contacts, she decided she needed to get to know her neighbourhood and did this by strolling up and down the seafront each morning. The story she told her grandchildren was about the day she met a lion roaming around on the local sea front.

On the morning in question, the young mother had taken her daughter on a route that passed a petrol station. Her attention was immediately captured by a hassled-looking man attempting to fill his car. The poor fellow seemed very distracted and agitated and kept calling out to their mother that she should take her pushchair away from the area as quickly as possible. He suggested that, if they were not careful, both mother and daughter might be eaten by a lion. Her immediate impression was that the fellow was drunk. What other conclusion could she come to? She added that she thought it was disgraceful that a gentleman should be so intoxicated that early in the day as to have fantasies about a lion on the prowl. Notwithstanding the distraction, she carried on with her walk, only to find that others in the area had the same dire warnings to relate. Quite a number rushed up the road and yelled out something about a lion. Finally, one particularly demented-looking woman rushed past and almost knocked down the woman and her baby. This passer-by looked desperate and was also crying out that there was a lion on the loose and it was just a short distance away down the road. Strangely, their stories turned out to be true. It seems that a circus was performing nearby; the lion-tamer had inadvertently left the cage door open and its occupant had escaped and mauled the trainer. The animal was now on the loose and was rambling around the neighbourhood.

Well, that story was like a light bulb going off in my head. In fact, it was manna from heaven to me. What had previously looked like being a very dull sermon would now have some meat to it. I loved the account, but wondered how I might use it during the liturgy. On returning to my community that evening, I recounted the tale to a community member who capped it off with an anecdote of his own. He mentioned that a baby lion lived with its mother in the zoo and was constantly telling its mother that everyone loved him. Why? Because great crowds came around their location and paused outside the lion cage to look adoringly in at the young cub. 'It's easy to see they love me,' was the way he put it to his mum, but the lioness didn't seem so sure. No matter how much the mother tried to dissuade the cub of its pious notion, the young fellow held doggedly to his theory. That's how matters stood until one day their keeper got careless. He left the cage door a tiny bit ajar and the youngster slipped out through the small opening and made his way down towards town. Before long he chanced upon an amorous young couple standing beside a lamp post, wrapped up in their thoughts and in each other. To gain their attention, the young cub rubbed himself up against their legs. As soon as they glanced down and saw who was beside them they began to scream in fright and terror. Half the neighbourhood was awakened by their roars as the pair high-tailed it out of there as quickly as their legs would carry them. More or less the same thing happened with the next two or three individuals the young lion encountered. No sooner was he noticed than wild screams of terror were emitted and those he was trying to befriend removed themselves from the scene with all possible haste.

So it was that the young lion had to return to his mother with tears in his eyes. 'They all hate me,' was all he could manage to blubber out between sobs, but again his mother seemed to have a different opinion. 'You're about as wrong in that conclusion as you were when you told me they all love you,' the mother told him. 'They don't hate you and neither do they love you. They just prefer it when you're behind bars.'

That little story packs a powerful message if we relate it to our own faith lives and that's what I hoped to get across during the funeral service. Anthony de Mello always displayed a great sense of inner freedom during the courses he gave and he tried to impart that same gift to those with whom he came in contact. At his retreats and workshops he wanted people to feel alert, alive and aware – not trapped behind bars. He taught participants how they might notice where, instead of shutting down their emotions, they might work out creative ways to move forward and get away from what had enslaved them. So when I began to speak at the funeral service, I settled on the idea that death is like a moving on from one place to another. In life, we sometimes have a feeling of being caged in, not being able to express ourselves as we might wish. I suspect de Mello felt that the worst type of religion can do this to us. If it tries to suffocate us and restrict the breath of the Spirit, something wonderful can die. Pope Francis has offered similar sentiments and his early interviews were sprinkled with wonderful vitality and verve. He seemed to be very much aware that if he did not seize the initiative early in his pontificate, his creativity might be snatched from him. The more institutional side of the Church might try to keep the lion firmly locked behind bars, so to speak.

Our habits and practices – both individually and as Church – may confine and ensnare Jesus. By being too 'precious', we – as individuals or as Church – may restrict his life-giving grace and Spirit. As 'Church', we may be so self-referential that we confine Jesus within the institutionalised structure and smother his energising presence.

Just like the lion in my funeral service, might Jesus be trying to get out of the door or out from behind the bars, instead of trying to get in? It's a sobering thought, and one that we might be well advised to ask about in our own lives too.

Irish Jesuit Michael Paul Gallagher, a master story-teller, liked to tell this anecdote. It concerned a young boy who had been brought up in an orphanage that was both austere and authoritarian. The inmates knew that you had better behave yourself in the establishment and that any deviation from the rules would be severely punished. One particular rule was paramount. Once you went to bed, you did not talk and did not get up for any reason during the night. As the young lad told his story to Fr Gallagher, he described one occasion when he woke up very early in the morning. It was still dark, with the first hint of sunlight just appearing. He could see the beams of light streaming in through the windows and a gorgeous golden haze suffusing the dormitory. The only word to describe the atmosphere was 'enchanting'.

Everybody was asleep and our story-teller knew it was a major offence to get out of bed. Something, however, impelled him upwards and he made his way to the window. Outside, the night was turning into day and the dew lay on the grass. Some distance away he could make out the silvery sheen of a lake behind some trees in the orphanage grounds. The beauty of the whole scene swept over him and he could not resist putting his coat on over his pyjamas. With great trepidation and noiseless as a mouse, he crept down the stairs. Some stern portraits of long-dead Christian Brothers looked down on him from their position on the wall, but he made it down as far as the back door without being discovered. When he told his tale to Fr Gallagher he said he could still remember the feeling of the dew-laden grass beneath his feet as he took the path to the shining lake. Once there, he felt perfect peace and settled on a log that had already been warmed by the morning sun. Golden reeds rose from the lakeside water and before long the tranquillity of his surroundings lulled him into a dreamy sleep. He wasn't sure how long this state held him in a trance but he does remember being rudely awakened from his slumbers by the sound of a bell. 'Getting up' time in the orphanage had arrived and with it the dreadful realisation that he was out of his bed and that discovery was almost inescapable. At that moment, he said, it suddenly dawned on him that there are, in reality, at least two faces of God. He described these as the 'God of the Orphanage' and the 'God of the Lake'. The first basically represented a God who rules with an iron fist, doles out punishments and keeps us behind bars. The 'God of the Lake', however, symbolised a God who releases, liberates and encourages us to be all that we can be and who, as it were, opens the cage and allows us to roam free. From now on – no matter what the cost – the lad told Fr Gallagher that he would give his allegiance to a God who liberates and not a God who suffocates.

So what sort of an image of God do I have?

It's interesting to go back in your mind to where, when and how your first image of God was formed. Who gave it to you and for what purpose? Many writers, including James Joyce or C. S. Lewis, have left us vivid descriptions of how and by whom they were given their early descriptions of the deity. It has to be said that the sort of representation of God that was painted for them in their youth was, in some instances, fairly horrendous. If that's the sort of image you have been given, it will obviously influence the way you pray. For our first prayer exercise, we'll try to look back and discover which face of God is the one we find ourselves saddled with.

To get yourself started, choose a place and time that works for you, somewhere you can be alone and undisturbed, and where you will not be bombarded with distractions.

Silence is generally a great help. If you are not used to being by yourself, or if you find the stillness a little threatening, you can use meditative music to soften the experience.* In a similar way, you may find it helpful to light a candle before you begin as this creates an atmosphere of devotion. Finally, you may like to sit, kneel, stand or lie down to create tranquillity within your body. Keep your back straight and slowly close your eyes.

Begin to observe your breath with its own particular pace and pattern. Without trying to change the pace, build up a good, steady rhythm. Do this by silently counting to four on each inbreath and again to four on each outbreath. Keep the tempo slow and regular. You might keep this up for two or three minutes until you have established a rhythm.

If your mind wanders, simply return to the business at hand by once again observing your breath.

Ask the Lord to be with you as a guide and mentor during this time of prayer.

Go back in your memory to the first person who formed an image of God for you. Who was it? I can think of my father sitting in a large armchair with a number of my brothers and sisters perched on the arms and looking over his shoulder as he read from a colourful book about the boy Jesus. The illustrations were wonderful, with pictures of Jesus, aged ten or so, working with Joseph. That's my first image of you, Lord.

I might stop to talk to you about the impact of those illustrations – or the stories about what you did with your parents, Mary and Joseph.

Do you have other reminiscences from your childhood that influenced your vision of what God is like and, if so, what are those memories?

When you feel ready, move forward in time because your image of God has now changed. Who do you now understand him to be? How did the change come about?

If you think of how you would now like him to be, what would that image look like?

There are two participants in this prayer exercise, so take a back seat for a while and leave space for the Spirit to intervene and for Jesus to communicate if he so desires in whatever way he might wish. Remember that in the Old and New Testament God communicates and takes the initiative. Remember the cases of Abraham, Moses and Samuel. Each was made an offer, but nothing much would have happened if those three individuals hadn't noticed God's presence nearby.

'Lord, I ask that I might be similarly alert here.'

End with the Lord's Prayer.

* At the back of this book you will find a list of music resources that I sometimes use and find helpful. Many groups I work with have said that the music somehow helps to settle them and keep them focused on the task at hand.

Encounters with the divine often engender fear.

Let's see what Our Lady can teach us about such an encounter.

> 'In the sixth month, the angel Gabriel was sent from God to a city of Galilee named Nazareth, to a virgin betrothed to a man whose name was Joseph, of the house of David; and the virgin's name was Mary. And he came to her and said, "Hail, O favoured one, the Lord is with you.' But she was greatly troubled at the saying, and considered in her mind what sort of greeting this might be. And the angel said to her, "Do not be afraid, Mary, for you have found favour with God. And behold you will conceive in your womb and bear a son and you shall call his name Jesus." … And Mary said to the angel, "How can this be, since I have no husband?" And the angel said to her, "The Holy Spirit will come upon you, and the power of the Most High will over-shadow you; therefore the child to be born will be called holy, the Son of God. And behold, your kinswoman Elizabeth in her old age has also conceived a son; and this is the sixth month with her who was called barren. For with God, nothing will be impossible." And Mary said, "Behold, I am the handmaid of the Lord; let it be done to me according to your word." And the angel departed from her.'

Place yourself with Our Lady in the scene described above.

Think of how Mary must have felt during these moments of confusion.

She has received a stupendous invitation, but what is she to make of it?

God begins the conversation with Mary, as he does with us, breaking into our lives in unexpected ways. The initiative lies entirely with God.

Feeling alone and vulnerable, Mary must have been terrified and unsure but the angel is at hand and helps her to discern.

Can you think of times in your life when you were faced with a decision that needed to be made?

As you recall the time and event in question, might you now be able – in retrospect – to see God's presence in the decision that was finally reached?

Has God been with us at difficult decisive times in the past?

Mary says 'yes' to a future she can neither yet see nor comprehend. She trusts and believes, even if the modern mind has difficulty believing in the miraculous. Such belief lies at the very heart of the gospels and highlights a gift we might well ask a share of ourselves.

As we sit with this passage, a note from Mother Teresa's journals (2007) may be of benefit to us. We might suppose that such a saintly figure would rarely be plagued with doubts about her faith but I know many people were shocked to discover when reading extracts from her diary after her death that this is exactly the fate that befell her in later life. She says that after a series of mystical experiences early in her adult life, the rest of her days passed with little sense of God's presence within her prayer. She had to contend with a sort of interior darkness, or a feeling of distance from God. She wrote that God seemed absent and her sufferings meaningless. Many of us believe that we alone struggle with prayer and listlessness and complain that we find prayer dull, dry or boring. We wonder if God is listening or if he hears us. Does God care at all and is prayer worth the effort? True holiness, Mother Teresa said, consists in doing God's will with a smile. If even the holiest individuals have times of darkness and doubt, we might be wise to make a prayerful request that the angel of reassurance stays at our side.

St Ignatius realised that different spirits move within us constantly. In fact, he tells us that if nothing was happening within his own prayer he got worried and begged God to take over and help him to become more aware.

Our job is to try and notice what's going on during our prayer time and what those 'movements of the spirit' that occur might be saying to us. Try to look at what is underpinning your moods and feelings.

Is there a particular desire? Is it your desire that you win, or become famous – or that God be honoured and served?

Note the general direction of your desires. What do you have to let go of to serve Jesus?

One way God often seems to speak to people in prayer is through their imaginations. By using your imagination to colour a particular gospel text or to look back over an incident that befell you in a new and challenging way, you may be helped to see what God is actually offering you or is calling you towards.

St Ignatius of Loyola often used imagination in a very innovative way in his prayer and experienced great emotional variations as he moved from periods of desolation right through to moments when he felt he was being gifted with an almost mystical sense of God in his life.

He mentions that the best spiritual directors are those who can help you discern where and if God is at work in your life. They may also be able to point out places or incidents where you might be tempted to act against God's will.

You are trying to discern in which direction the Spirit might be leading you and St Ignatius gives very concrete examples from his own life. The account below is one of the better known instances where he spells this out from personal experience.

As he lay recuperating from his battle injuries, Ignatius had time to reflect and notice what was going on in his interior life. You might say he had little choice. He was confined to bed and had little option but to be still and quiet. He did, however, make good use of the situation he found himself having to endure.

Each day, he alternated between daydreaming and reading. After these different activities of reading and fantasising, he was able to notice that he went through a variety of moods. After thinking about worldly thoughts and activities for a good length of time, he noticed that he felt elated – but only for a short time. Afterwards, he felt tired and flat. That was telling him something, but what exactly was it saying?

Next he moved on to daydreaming about doing something wonderful for God. He imagined himself setting out for Jerusalem on a godly mission – a journey that would entail rigours and perils. You might suppose that this would have filled his heart with dread and revulsion. However, not only was this not the case, but even after he put these dreams aside he continued, to his surprise, to remain content and happy. He concluded from these experiences that some thoughts left him sad and others left him happy. Slowly he came to recognise the difference between the spirits that moved him and concluded that one set of feelings came from the enemy and the other from God. If you use your imagination with a gospel passage such as the Prodigal Son (Lk 15) you may get a very practical example of this for yourself.

We've tried this passage before (at the end of Chapter 6) but, this time, just sit with the younger son and see what happens to him.

'There was a man who had two sons; and the younger of them said to his father, "Father, give me the share of property that falls to me." And he divided his living between them. Not many days later the younger son gathered all he had and took his journey into a far country, and there he squandered his property in loose living. And when he had spent everything, a great famine arose in that country, and he began to be in want. So he went and joined himself to one of the citizens of that country, who sent him into his fields to feed swine. And he would gladly have fed on the pods that the swine ate; and no one gave him anything. But when he came to himself he said, "How many of my father's hired servants have bread enough and to spare but I perish here with hunger! I will arise and go to my father and I will say to him, 'Father, I have sinned against heaven and before you; I am no longer worthy to be called your son; treat me as one of your hired servants.'" And he arose and came to his father. But while he was yet at a distance, his father saw him and had compassion, and ran and embraced him and kissed him. And the son said to him, "Father, I have sinned before heaven and against you; I am no longer worthy to be called your son." But the father said to his servants, "Bring quickly the best robe, and put it on him; and put a ring on his hand and shoes on his feet; and bring the fatted calf and kill it, and let us eat and make merry; for this my son was dead, and is alive again; he was lost, and is found." And they began to make merry.

Now his elder son was in the fields and as he came and drew near to the house, he heard music and dancing. And he called one of the servants and asked him what this meant. And the servant said to him, "Your brother has come, and your father has killed the fatted calf, because he has received him safe and sound." But he was angry and refused to go in. His father came out and entreated him, but he answered his father, "Lo, these many years I have served you, and I never disobeyed your command; yet you never gave me a kid that I might make merry with my friends. But when this son of yours came, who has devoured your living with harlots, you killed for him the fatted calf!" And he said to him, "Son, you are always with me, and all that is mine is yours. It was fitting to make merry and be glad, for your brother was dead and is alive; he was lost, and is found.'"

As soon as the younger son departs his father's house, changes occur pretty quickly in his life. He is now his own master but a very unwise one. He spends and wastes, throwing away an inheritance that had been put together for him by somebody else.

Just one sentence tells us so much. 'After a while he came to his senses.'

What you want to do at this point is to try and find how he came to his senses. Was he helped by an outside force to see himself and his actions in a new light? If so, who or what was that outside force?

The story clearly illustrates that the younger son makes an abrupt about-turn at this juncture. Were his own prayers or the prayers of his father instrumental in this conversion?

As you mull over any issues that may need to be resolved in your own life, ask the Spirit of Enlightenment to clarify your options as to the best way forward for you.

Finish with the Lord's Prayer.

12

HIGH FINANCE

All men should strive before they die, to work out what they are
running from, and to, and why.
James Thurber

I have a friend whose father was a well-known writer. One of his tasks was to write a weekly column for one of our national newspapers and, as you might imagine, dreaming up fresh ideas each week to keep his readers entertained really put a strain on his initiative. As deadline dates drew near, his efforts to dredge up something new and exciting often bordered on the frantic. One incident particularly stands out in my friend's memory and has stayed with her for the best part of fifty years.

As a child, my friend had a post office savings book which had been given to her to teach her something about looking after her own finances. On the occasion in question, the savings book had only ten old pence in it (that tells you something about how long ago all this happened) but the young lady had spotted a lovely doll in a local shop that cost exactly that amount of money and she was very keen to acquire it. Before it was snapped up by somebody else she went down to take out her savings and make the purchase. Imagine her surprise when the postmistress informed her that the lowest withdrawal one could make from an account was one shilling (twelve pence). Now it seems to me that most ten-year-olds would have given up at that point, but that's not exactly my friend's style. She approached her Dad and asked if she could borrow sixpence from him. She also promised to repay the loan that very same day. I imagine the poor man was a bit perplexed – not to say intrigued – about how his daughter was going to achieve this feat of borrowing, spending and reimbursing all in the same day. However, he kept his doubts to himself and shelled out the money. Without saying what she was up to, his daughter marched down to the post office and put the sixpence into her account. With sufficient funds to make a withdrawal, she drew out one shilling and four pence. She then proceeded to buy her doll, repay the sixpence debt to her father, and went on to explain why she had needed his money to top up her account in the first place. He was so intrigued by her methods that he first mentioned the possibility of her becoming the next finance minister of the country. He then said she would certainly be an improvement on the present holder of the office, and wrote up an account of her monetary acumen for his newspaper column that very evening, giving it the title 'High Finance'. She claims that he even paid her one shilling for the 'property rights' to the idea. Her father knew that when one gets a bit low on creativity, all scribes have to glean new material from any source that presents itself. My friend remembered the lesson that this incident in her early life had taught her, and you might have a similar memory of an important youthful life lesson.

Reminiscences from childhood leave an indelible impression. They provide guidelines that help in later life and many writers make use of these recollections as they get older. I do this myself, and if you had to work up an article or sermon at short notice fairly regularly, I suspect you might use same tactic yourself. Thus, when my friend told me her anecdote about balancing out her post office account, it sparked off something in me. I remembered a vaguely similar incident when I was given a lesson about the moral and financial worlds and their perils. This event happened many years ago but the memory is still very vivid and, I suspect, always will be. It features the Grand National in Liverpool, England, and in case you don't know what the Grand National is, I should explain that it's a major horse race that takes place once a year. The animals have to jump about thirty enormous fences and this usually results in all kinds of mayhem. Horses come crashing down one after the other and the whole extravaganza makes for a huge spectacle. I've always thought of it as one of the highlights of the sporting calendar and I think I was bitten by the bug when I was about twelve.

I should explain – before anyone gets the wrong impression – that my family didn't bet on horses. Never have, and hopefully never will. The very thought of any of us being seen inside a betting shop would have carried with it everlasting shame in my household. However, the year in question, I was rather captivated by the name of one of the animals that had been entered for the Grand National. The horse was called Merryman II and nothing would do me but to lay a wager on him. Of course I had never been to a betting shop and, to complicate matters further, my pocket money was so low that I knew I needed a backer if the venture was to have any chance. It was at that point that I inveigled my younger brother to join the scheme. Our combined assets would just be sufficient to cover the minimum bet. Also, I knew a local lad a little older than either of us – but a good deal more worldly-wise – who would know his way around a betting shop, and, I assured my brother, he could and would put down the bet for us.

You always get pretty decent odds when betting on the Grand National because, in truth, the race is a real lottery and your chances of winning are slim. That year, however, our luck was in. Merryman II ran like the wind and – with a shilling of mine riding on its back – romped home well ahead of the field. Things got even better when one of the race commentators gave us a blow-by-blow description of how events had unfolded and relayed the news that my animal's starting price was fifteen to one. It meant that we had won fifteen shillings – a small fortune to me – and I couldn't wait to drag my young brother quietly down the road so that we could collect our winnings without attracting any attention at home.

It's amazing how quickly a person's situation can change from boom to bust or hero to zero and I still remember the great feeling of anticipation and inner warmth as I contemplated how I might dispose of my winnings. Almost before that feeling had taken root, however, it was replaced with a horrible hollowness in the pit of my stomach when the moment of the cash handover arrived. The lad we had given our shilling to and who had offered to place the bet, was clearly a lot more savvy than I. As I put out my hand for our winnings, he looked me in the eye and, without the slightest blush of shame, said that he hadn't had time to actually place the bet. With that, he put his hand in his pocket and returned the shilling I had entrusted to him. Even now, years and years after the event, I can feel the shame and loathing that sprang up in me – for I strongly suspect that my youthful neighbour had never had any intention of putting down the bet but fully intended to pocket our money when our horse lost. He anticipated making a small 'killing' of a shilling from two young 'suckers' when their horse became an also-ran. He had also dreamed up a way of covering himself in the unlikely event that our animal did manage to make it over the finishing line by the simple expedient of a lie. All he had to do was insist that he hadn't had time to get to the bookies.

The incident, I need hardly add, left a bad taste in my mouth for ages afterwards. It was, however, a sort of black cloud with a silver lining as it provided a cheap tutorial in 'high finance' that I might, in other circumstances, have paid more harshly to receive. Its message was, 'Be careful who you do business with', and I suspect the message may well be as applicable today as it was that Grand National day.

Trying to decide who to do business with and working out what sort of person might be a reliable guide is important not only in worldly affairs but also in matters of faith. Not all guides are equally reliable and some are deadly dangerous. Ignatius of Loyola was forever pointing out that there are 'good spirits' hovering around to offer guidance and good counsel if we ask for it, but he was equally adamant – and so was Anthony de Mello – that 'spirits' of a much less wholesome variety are also active and roaming around to catch the unwary and we need to be on our guard if they are not to wreak havoc in our affairs. In *The Screwtape Letters* C. S. Lewis illustrates this point perfectly with one of his stories. He depicts a scene from hell and paints a picture of a senior devil giving lessons to a couple of apprentices in how to lead people astray on earth. As an assignment or test for these junior devils, the higher-ranking demon asked what tactic they would use to point individuals towards the road to hell. The first trainee said he would try to convince his adversary that there was no hell. That would make the individual concerned very lax. The second junior devil said he would go about convincing his antagonist that there was no heaven, as that would take away the fellow's hope. The third novice was the one who received the greatest accolade from his teacher, for he said that he would try to convince the person in his charge that there was no need to hurry or worry about speedily making any changes in one's life. Better to put things off. Procrastinate. Wouldn't tomorrow be just as good as today when it comes to trying to effect transformation? And that's exactly what St Ignatius used to say – that the devil has many strategies. To knock us off our stride he proposes a strategy of attachment to wealth, honours and vain pride. Satan's goal is to enslave people. He wants us to concentrate on worldly things rather than heavenly things. Jesus' lifestyle is exactly the opposite. His strategy is detachment from wealth, honours and pride. By this strategy Jesus hopes to free people from the binds of earthly ties. He knew too well from his own experience of grappling with Satan during his temptations in the desert that many different tests are likely to come our way. By refusing to turn stones into bread Jesus indicated that he would not use his power for his own personal comfort. By refusing to throw himself from the Temple, he showed that he hadn't come to be served but to serve. By not allowing himself to kneel down before the devil he signalled that he was unwilling to bargain with evil or to have any truck with it. Jesus will die at the hands of evil rather than compromise with it.

As we try to see how our lives are panning out at the moment, it may be wise to ask what deeper needs – above bread alone – are revealing themselves. How might I satisfy those needs and do I sometimes tend to barter with evil rather than stay far away from it? All contact with real wickedness has a tendency to corrode whether we like it or not and it often does so insidiously. An image comes to mind here from Naples, where they have an unusual type of jellyfish that one needs to be wary of. They are attracted to a type of snail found locally and they try to eat these. They quickly find that they are biting off more than they can chew, for these snails have particularly hard shells – and as soon as they are consumed the interior damage begins. The jellyfish finds that the shells of the snail cannot be digested. Worse still, the tiny organism now begins to eat the jellyfish from the inside. Unless the jellyfish manages to vomit up the snail, the tiny creature inside it will eventually bring about its destruction. It's not a pleasant image but it may help us to do a bit of self-examination. Do we have any habits that eat us up from the inside?

Questions like these are not easy to grapple with, but I've been greatly encouraged by the way Pope Francis has engaged in this sort of self-searching question since his election to the papacy. Almost as soon as he was elected, he conducted a series of interviews that I find very revealing. He knows that everybody blunders as they make their way through life and humbly admits that he is no exception. Reflecting back over his early years as a Jesuit, he says simply and with great honesty, 'I made terrible mistakes. I damaged people. I made decisions in the wrong way.' He knows that he was young at the time and was placed in leadership roles without much personal life experience but does not excuse himself because of that. People in his care were hurt, and, in retrospect, perhaps unnecessarily. If he had consulted more widely and with more experienced confrères before he jumped into action some of the mistakes might have been avoided. It's that willingness to look back with bravery on his own methods that now permits him to see himself through new eyes.

As we pray, we also hope that our past may help us see with new eyes, and so we ask for insights and honesty such as those displayed by Francis. If personal decisions or adaptations need to be made, we ask for bravery and wisdom in making those changes. St Ignatius of Loyola asks us to take time out occasionally to see if, and where, we may have strayed off course. When deciding how best to move forward, he suggests we first try to ascertain if there is some clarity about what God wants us to do. If there is, the wisest course of action is often reasonably clear. All that is required is our willingness to take the first step. However, it may be that the possible options before us paint a confused picture and that can easily create a good deal of agitation. The person having to make a decision cannot remain frozen in indecision, even if procrastination is often our preferred method of dealing with the predicament. St Ignatius was a great believer in 'looking back' in such situations to see if any similar issue had raised its head before. Look at how you dealt with the problem then, and see if your way of proceeding brought peace of mind and satisfactory results – or if it did not. Such knowledge is often a good guide in regard to your natural strengths and weaknesses and dictates how best you might proceed with resolving your present dilemma. Sometimes you may have to face situations when there is neither clarity nor good counsel near at hand and the following may help.

Clarify what exactly are the decisions you must make and which choices lie before you.

Recall that your decision should be in accordance with God's purpose in creating the world. You were created so that you could share your life and love with God and with other people.

Pray for the grace to be open to the right choice.

List the pros and cons for each course of action that is open to you.

Determine which route seems to accord more with God's purpose in creating you.

Make your decision, asking God to confirm it.

Ask yourself if the inner movements you feel stem from your love of God or from some other source such as selfishness or pride.

Imagine you are a person you have never met before. You take a liking to this person and want the best for him or her. Ask yourself what you would advise this person to do if he or she had to make the same decision that you have to make.

Imagine yourself at the moment of death. Ask yourself which choice would likely give you greater joy if you looked back at it at that time.

Imagine yourself before the judgment seat of God after your death and ask yourself to view your decision from that vantage point.

EXERCISE ONE: DISCERNING THE BEST WAY FORWARD FOR YOU

Take a real-life dilemma that you may have had to tackle within the last two or three years. It may be that you wondered whether you should take up a particular line of study, or change from your present occupation to a new situation or move on from a relationship you are unsure about.

St Ignatius recommended trying to find out God's will for you and called this practice 'discernment'. It's not as easy as it might at first appear. It involves trying to get to know more fully the will of God – for me. We might describe it as the point at which one's head and heart come together.

Some of the university students I worked with found the following system useful. If they were faced with particular dilemmas regarding which line of action they should pursue during their years of study, this technique was coherent and reasonably easy to follow.

Let us suppose they were involved in a relationship but were vaguely uneasy with either the direction the liaison was taking or the speed at which it was developing. First they would take sheets of paper and draw out a sort of grid. After that they would spell out for themselves the real options they had with regard to the question they were facing and any concrete alternatives that were available to them.

The Issue

Should you continue to give yourself fully to a relationship you are unsure about or might it be better to break it up now?

Fill out each column with whatever thoughts come to mind. For example, the advantages to be gained from continuing in the relationship might be as follows:

- It postpones having to make a decision.
- It avoids the pain of a break-up.
- My partner will not be severely hurt.
- It avoids the risk of losing someone I really like.

The disadvantages in not grasping the nettle now are:

- We continue on with no real decision made.
- There is no clean break.
- It prevents me starting new relationships.
- My studies are suffering because of the indecision and will continue to do so.

What advantages are likely
to be gained by continuing
in the relationship?

....

....

....

....

What disadvantages are
likely to result if I continue
on in this relationship?

....

....

....

....

You will probably find that a number of very similar points will make their appearance in both columns – but take time to check out how you feel about each option as you reflect on what you have written. In your imagination, think about what you would feel if you had opted for one course of action rather than the other. If, for example, you had broken up the relationship and it was already over, would you now feel relieved or devastated? Often it is easier to get a handle on how you would feel as you look back on a decision already made and executed rather than anticipate the feelings created before the reality checks in. The students I worked with might have to spend quite some time chewing over the situation they found themselves in before coming up with salient points to flesh out their columns. They went to their room or even a prayer space and closed the door. They created the conditions for inner peace and tried to let their cares and immediate concerns fade into the background. Sometimes they used a Taizé chant or a decade of the Rosary to soothe their inner worries and they relaxed into God's presence as they tried to surrender and let the Spirit guide them. Slowly points both for and against the different courses of action began to emerge and these were jotted down to be reflected upon. Not unusually, it was noted that there were advantages and disadvantages to whichever course of action was selected. After a while one of the columns begins to gather a significant number of points even if the course of action selected turned out not to be without drawbacks – and it's important to remember that probably any way forward that you select is likely to leave some regrets. To help us understand that last point, I remember Irish novelist Maeve Binchy saying that we never get everything we want from life. As her book *Tara Road* was being filmed, friends asked if she was happy about how the movie was panning out. 'I think it's a balance,' she said. Nobody has everything at the same time. When you're young, you have time and energy but you don't have any money. When you get a job, you have energy and money but you don't have time. When you finally head towards middle age, you have time and you have money but you don't have the energy you require. Nobody has all three together.

So, notwithstanding the possible downsides, I try to move forward, noting the observations in the grid and then putting the matter into the hands of God. If things still seem very confused and if I do have a bit more time, I may decide to let the matter rest for a while and come back to it in prayer at a later date.

Anthony de Mello liked to use a particular meditation during his three-month Indian Sadhana courses on prayer. To try it for yourself, you have to put together an imaginary scene.

You have been invited to a local art gallery or museum where a statue of yourself has recently been created and is due for unveiling today. So set out with your personal invitation. Probably you are excited, though you may also be a bit apprehensive and you have some questions.

What kind of a statue will you find?

Will you like the representation?

Do you have pre-judged notion of what the sculpture will be like?

Is it large or small, made of wood, stone, bronze or something else entirely?

Is there any particular aspect of the figure before you that is a surprise to you?

What is that surprise element?

One person I know who took on this imaginative exercise was shocked when they went into the viewing room. They were obviously skilled at using their imagination, for they discovered a pile of white sand on the pedestal where they expected their statue to be. About the same time as they noticed the sand, they also noticed the person of Jesus coming into the viewing area. As soon as Christ spotted the sand, he scooped it up into his hands. Instead of being disgusted or disappointed with what he found, Jesus seemed pleased. The sand particles represented light and beauty to him and allowed the Lord to recreate in a new and glorious way the one being viewed. Instead of the moment being one of disillusionment, it was instead a major boost to the viewer's ego.

So now use your own imagination to think of Jesus coming to stand beside you and share in the viewing of your statue.

Talk with him about your own impression of what the artist has produced.

Mention what you are happy about and also any blemishes you notice.

Then go into listening mode to see if Jesus has any contribution to make to the discussion.

As he affirmed so many of those he met on a daily basis around Galilee, Jesus may well want first to affirm you.

He may also want to let you see where growth and development might be possible as you move towards the future.

Finish with the Lord's Prayer.

Remember Jesus' parable of the mustard seed. Although tiny when planted in the soil, it makes great progress and increases greatly in size and strength.

First, imagine a tiny mustard seed being placed in the soil.
Who does the planting and what are their expectations?
Ask the seed to tell you its story.

'I remember the beginning which is very hazy in my mind but I do recall that the soil was dark and cold.

At first nothing much seemed to be happening in my life ... but change takes time.

Almost without my noticing, things seemed to happen. Suddenly, I could feel something moving within me. I was being drawn upwards by some invisible force.

Now I can just make out a vague sense of the gloom lifting and a certain light coming into my surroundings.

Other creatures are moving around close to where I am positioned, but whether they are similar beings to me or are made from a completely different mould is hard to tell.

Now my twigs are just beginning to break the surface of the soil and I can feel heat and sense real light for the first time.

I am emerging into a new environment, and I needed a new environment to prosper. Time and new circumstances are producing change, and as I think of myself in the soil I can sense development and transformation happening.

Progress may be slow, but when I finally break the surface of the soil I immediately sense the quantity, quality and effect of the light and heat taking effect on my being.

I notice uppermost parts break through the surface, I notice other seeds have already broken through and are now pushing upwards towards the sky.

It consoles me to know that I am not alone. There are others around to give encouragement and hint at what I may be able to achieve.'

Talk to the tree about the stages it has found itself going through and then talk to Jesus.

Ask if – in some way – the seed or tree mirrors your growth as a human being and a Christian.

'Jesus and his disciples went as far as Capernaum, and as soon as the Sabbath came he went to the synagogue and began to teach. And his teaching made a deep impression on them because, unlike the scribes, he taught them with authority.

In their synagogue just then there was a man possessed by an unclean spirit, and it shouted, "What do you want with us, Jesus of Nazareth? Have you come to destroy us? I know who you are; the Holy one of God." But Jesus said sharply, "Be quiet! Come out of him!" And the unclean spirit threw the man into convulsions and with a loud cry went out of him. The people were so astonished that they started asking each other what it all meant. "Here is a teaching that is new," they said, "and with authority behind it; he gives orders even to unclean spirits and they obey him." And his reputation rapidly spread everywhere, throughout all the surrounding Galilean countryside.'

Start by spending a little time with the man possessed by an unclean spirit. A number of facts might strike you and give you pause for consideration.

First of all, the man realises that he has a problem.

At one and the same time he appears to want to stay away from the light and still feels impelled to come close to Jesus. He seems to fear the implications of his actions but is even more afraid that the darkness may overwhelm him. To a certain extent he brings his dilemma to Jesus. Can you be equally brave?

Start by trying to spell out exactly what you think your problem is. (Getting that question right is usually the first step.)

Why is the concern you have noted a problem? (For the man in the gospel passage, the fact that an evil spirit has taken up residence within him is clearly affecting his life.)

Next, list the possible solutions to your problem. What steps forward are open to you? This may take time and at first nothing may come to mind. Persevere.

Jot down the advantages and disadvantages of each forward course of action you have come up with. (In the story, the man has taken definite action by going to Jesus. If something positive is done for him he needs to be careful that the evil spirit, if disturbed, does not return with a vengeance.)

Remind yourself that God is a partner in this endeavour. He may well inspire some impulse or way forward in your mind or heart about how best you might move forward.

Remind yourself that Jesus invited us to bring our worries to the Father.

Try not to hurry the Lord, or push too vigorously for a resolution.

Some requests are answered less speedily than we might wish, or in ways not to our liking.

An answer may not even come during the time of meditation but rather rise up through your unconscious mind on a later occasion when you are engaged in some other activity. It may leap from the page of a book, or suddenly reveal itself in the words of a friend, or make its appearance in that halfway state between waking and sleeping late at night or early in the morning.

Pray that your inner mind might be unclogged so that God can get his answer through to you.

How do you know that the solution presenting itself is from God? St Ignatius used to say that sometimes a response is clear and unambiguous but more often it isn't. He also said that it's easier to see in retrospect whether the course of action we've taken has been for the best or not.

By engaging in this practice of bringing your problems to God fairly regularly, you will increase your ability to see patterns and trends that have shown themselves during previous decision-making times. Insights gained in this way about how you react under pressure can be remarkably helpful in guiding you when fresh predicaments arise.

MUSIC TO ASSIST WITH MEDITATION PRACTICE

Celestial Guardian, Philip Chapman, New World Cassettes, Paradise Farm, Westhall, Halesworth, Suffolk,1990.

Reverence, Terry Oldfield, New World Cassettes, 1987.

The Fairy Ring, Mike Rowland, New World Cassettes, 1982.

The Healer, Seamus Byrne, S.O.L. Productions Ltd, Quarantine Hill, Wicklow, 1992.

(All the music resources listed are available on CD or for download.)

ADDITIONAL RESOURCES

BOOKS BY ANTHONY DE MELLO SJ

Contact with God, Retreat Conferences, Gujarat Sahitya Prakash, Anand, 1990.
One Minute Wisdom, Gujarat Sahitya Prakash, Anand, 1985.
Taking Flight, Doubleday, New York, 1988.
The Heart of the Enlightened, Collins Fount Paperbacks, London,1989.
The Prayer of the Frog, Gujarat Sahitya Prakash, Anand, I1988.
The Song of the Bird, Gujarat Sahitya Prakash, Anand, 1987, 1984.
Sadhana, A Way to God, Gujarat Sahitya Prakash, Anand, 1978.
Awareness, Doubleday, New York, 1990.
Call to Love, Gujarat Sahitya Prakash, Anand, 1991.
One-Minute Nonsense, Gujarat Sahitya Prakash, Anand, 1992.
The Way to Love. The Last Meditations of Anthony de Mello, Doubleday, New York, 1991.
Walking on Water, Crossroad Publishing Company, New York, 1998.
Wellsprings. A Book of Spiritual Exercises, Gujarat Sahitya Prakash, Anand, 1984.

VIDEO MATERIAL BY ANTHONY DE MELLLO SJ

Wake Up. Spirituality for Today, with Tony de Mello SJ, Tabor Publishing, Texas.
A Way to God for Today, with Tony de Mello SJ, Tabor Publishing, Texas.
Re-discovery of Life, Tony de Mello SJ, Available from Veritas, Dublin.

AUDIO MATERIAL BY ANTHONY DE MELLO SJ

Sadhana, We and God Spirituality Centre, St Louis University, St Louis, Missouri, 1989.
Wake Up To Life, We and God Spirituality Centre, St Louis University, St Louis, Missouri, 1989.

Wellsprings, We and God Spirituality Centre, St Louis University, St Louis, Missouri, 1989.

De Mello Satellite Retreat, We and God Spirituality Centre, St Louis University, St Louis, Missouri, 1989.

Barry, William A., SJ, *Paying Attention to God. Discernment in Prayer*, Ave Maria Press, Notre Dame, Indiana, 1990.

Barry, William A., SJ, and Connolly, William J., SJ, *Finding God in All Things. A Companion to the Spiritual Exercises*, Ave Maria Press, Notre Dame, Indiana, 2009.

Bozarath, Alla Renee, PhD, *A Journey through Grief*, Hazelden Publications, Minnesota, 1990.

Brunton, Paul, PhD, *A Search in Secret India*, Rider and Company, London, 1934.

Brys, Aurel, SJ, *We Heard the Bird Sing*, Gujarat Sahitya Prakash, Anand, 1995.

Callanan, John, SJ, *Dreaming with Tony de Mello*, Mercier Press, Cork, 1997.

Callanan, John, SJ, *Finding Fire with Tony de Mello*, Mercier Press, Cork, 2001.

Callanan, John, SJ, *Watering the Desert with Tony de Mello*, Mercier Press, Cork, 2004.

Carington, Patricia, PhD, *The Book of Meditation*, Element Publishers, Boston, Massachusetts, 1998.

Chilson, Richard W., *Meditation*, Sorin Books, Notre Dame, Indiana, 2004.

Coelho, Paulo, *By the river Piedra I sat down and wept*, Harper Perennial, New York, 1994.

Cooke, Grace, *Meditation*, The White Eagle Publishing Trust, 1955.

Davis, Roy Eugene, *An Easy Guide to Meditation*, Mercier Press, Cork, 1988.

Dyke, William, SJ, *Selected Readings of Anthony de Mello*, Orbis Books, Maryknoll, New York, 1999.

Fontana, David, *The Elements of Meditation*, Element Books, Dorset, 1991.

Green, Thomas H., SJ, *The Practice of Spiritual Direction*, The Seabury Press, New York, 1982.

Hebblethwaite, Margaret, *Weeds Among the Wheat. Discernment where Prayer and Action Meet*, Ave Maria Press, Notre Dame, Indiana, 1984.

Hughes, Gerard, SJ, *God of Surprises*, Darton, Longman & Todd, London, 1986.

Kennedy, Robert E., *Zen Spirit, Christian Spirit*, The Continuum International Publishing Group Inc., New York, 1995.

Kornfield, Jack, *Meditation for Beginners*, Bantam Books, London, 2004.

Lonsdale, David, SJ, *Eyes to See, Ears to Hear. An Introduction to Ignatian Spirituality*, Darton, Longman & Todd, London, 1990.

Mariani, Paul, *Thirty Days: On Retreat with the Exercises of St Ignatius*, Viking Compass Press/Penguin Random House, New York, 2002.

Maryland Province of the Society of Jesus, *Place Me With Your Son. The Spiritual Exercises in Everyday Life*, Maryland, 1985.

McVerry, Peter, SJ, *The God of Mercy, The God of the Gospels*, Veritas Publications, Dublin, 2016.

Merton, Thomas, *The Wisdom of the Desert*, New Directions Publications, New York, 1960.

Puhl, Louis J., SJ, *Spiritual Exercises of Saint Ignatius*, based on Studies in the Language of the Autograph, Loyola University Press, Chicago, 1951.

Pungente, John, SJ, and Williams, Monty, SJ, *Finding God in the Dark*, Novalis Press, Ottawa, 2004.

Schiffmann, Erich, *The Spirit and Practice of Moving into Stillness*, Pocket Books, New York, 1996.

Valles, Carlos G., SJ, *Unencumbered by Baggage*, Gujarat Sahitya Prakash, Anand, 1988.

Wilson, Paul, *The Calm Technique*, Thorsons, London, 1987.

Yancey, Philip, *Prayer*, Zondervan Publishing, Grand Rapids, Michigan, 2006.

Zanzig, Thomas, *Learning to Meditate*, Saint Mary's Press, Winona, Minnesota,1990.

AUDIO RESOURCES ON THE WORK OF

ANTHONY DE MELLO

Callanan, John, SJ, *Lighting the Fire. Prayer in the style of Anthony de Mello*, A boxed set of two audio cassette tapes, Cathedral Books, Dublin, 2003.

Callanan, John, SJ, The Spirit of Anthony de Mello. An introduction to Prayer and Meditation, A boxed set of four cassette tapes, Cathedral Books, Dublin, 1993.